FAMILY LITERACY STORYTIMES

*Readymade
storytimes
suitable for
the whole
family*

Kathryn Totten

Neal-Schuman Publishers, Inc.

New York   London

Published by Neal-Schuman Publishers, Inc.
100 William St., Suite 2004
New York, NY 10038

Printed and bound in the United States of America.

The paper used in this publication meets the minimum requirements of American National Standard for Information Sciences—Permanence of Paper for Printed Library Materials, ANSI Z39.48-1992.

Library of Congress Cataloging-in-Publication Data

Totten, Kathryn, 1955-
  Family literacy storytimes : readymade storytimes suitable for the whole family / Kathryn Totten.
    p. cm.
  Includes bibliographical references and index.
  ISBN 978-1-55570-671-5 (alk. paper)
  1. Libraries and families—United States. 2. Family literacy programs—United States. 3. Reading—Parent participation. 4. Children's libraries—Activity programs—United States. 5. Storytelling—United States. I. Title.

Z711.92.F34T68 2009
027.62'51—dc22

                                                                                    2009027770

Dedication

To all the families who use public libraries and bookmobiles

Table of Contents

Preface

Family Literacy Storytimes is designed to help librarians and others who program for young children and their caregivers quickly offer interactive storytime programs that will build literacy skills for children and their parents. The programs that follow are both educational and fun. You can use them to provide your community with opportunities for building oral fluency in English, expose them to quality children's literature, and provide everyone with a memorable experience that will foster lifelong reading, learning, and library use. The storytime plans in this book build on traditional stories, but they contain an important added value: language instruction.

According to the National Center for Family Literacy, "Family literacy teaches families that they can learn together, that learning is a mutual process . . . [and] that learning is fun" (National Center for Family Literacy, accessed 2008). When parents actively participate in storytimes, they are learning the skills that they need to be their child's first teacher. By example, they are showing their child reading is important. Through participation in family storytime, parents acquire knowledge and skills that allow them to repeat the experience at home. This is beneficial for English-language learners, and the parent and the child, since learning a new language requires a great deal of repetition. Family storytime is offered at many libraries in addition to an array of preschool programs. In a traditional storytime, children participate while their parents or caregivers stand aside or wait outside the room or story area. When both adults and children of all ages (younger children and their older siblings) participate, the same material and experience have value on multiple levels. School-aged children enjoy the familiarity of picture books, which they enjoyed when they were younger. Rob Reid observes, "the children may laugh or express astonishment at one point in the story, while adults react to other parts" (Reid, 1999: 2). Family literacy storytimes also facilitate teaching between parent and child, in both directions. Often, children pick up a language easier than an adult. When the experience is shared, the whole family can build language skills together.

Family Literacy Storytimes is a complete tool for librarians who prepare storytimes. Part I explains the purpose of *Family Literacy Storytimes* and offers suggestions that will help both adults and children to acquire language proficiency. Chapter 1 explains the acute need for family literacy programs and offers ways that public and school libraries can help in this area. Suggestions for meeting the needs of both the adult and the child in family literacy storytimes are given in Chapters 2, 3, and 4. Chapter 5 covers the basics such as creating a storytime space, using a standard opening and closing activity, and the use of visual aids. Chapter 6 outlines the six pre-literacy skills identified by the Public Library Association that children can begin learning from birth (Public Library Association, 2004). Chapter 7 provides a list of organizations that support family literacy at the national, state, and local level.

Part II features program components. Chapter 8 includes ideas for planning a storytime with a family literacy focus. Original songs, traditional rhymes and rhyming stories with patterns are included in Chapters 9, 10, and 11. These can be used as connecting activities and also can be given to families to take home, to extend the experience. Finally, Chapter 12 includes 25 storytime themes. A select annotated list of recently published picture books is included for each; a reference to which of the six pre-reading skills can be demonstrated with each book is included. Several activities for extended learning are included for each selected book. This is an important element of *Family Literacy Storytimes,* because it offers repetition and vocabulary building that is focused by subject. Suggestions for standard opening and closing activities are given. Each theme includes a sample plan for a 30-minute program. The original songs, action rhymes, and stories with patterns, and literacy activities are designed to help you offer family literacy programming that will both build your community's literacy skills as well as provide engaging activities at the library.

REFERENCES

National Center for Family Literacy. "What Is Family Literacy?". Available: www.famlit.org (accessed November 12, 2008).

Public Library Association. "Every Child Ready to Read @ Your Library: Parent Guide to Early Literacy for Pre-Readers." (2004). Available: www.pla.org/earlyliteracy.htm (accessed November 12, 2008).

Reid, Rob. 1999. *Family Storytime: Twenty-four Creative Programs for All Ages.* Chicago, IL: American Library Association.

PART I

FAMILY LITERACY STORYTIME BASICS

Chapter 1

The Purpose of Family Literacy Storytimes

THE NEED FOR FAMILY LITERACY PROGRAMS

The purpose of the Family Literacy Storytime is to provide literacy support at public libraries. It provides a foundation of English fluency and pre-literacy skills before children go to school, and gives parents the confidence and skills needed to teach their children. Libraries are a free and available resource for families. In many cases, they are the only source to early childhood literacy education. The need for family literacy programs is acute, especially among low-income families. According to the National Center for Family Literacy, "by age four children from poor families will have heard 32 million fewer words than children living in professional families. In the United States, one in five of children age 5 and under live in poverty. There are over 30 million adults in the United States with extremely low literacy skills" (National Center for Family Literacy, 2008). Middle-income families are also at risk, because they generally cannot afford private preschools and do not qualify for national- or state-funded programs. Research finds that many middle-income children start school significantly behind. For some of them, this causes lasting problems. About 1 in 10 children from middle-income families fail a grade or drop out of high school. Research shows that pre-literacy education reduces later dropout rates and repeating of grades (NIEER, 2007).

LIBRARIES MEET LITERACY NEEDS OF THE COMMUNITY

In the United States, public libraries are available in almost every neighborhood. According to the ALA Library Fact Sheet 1, in April of 2008 there were 16,543 public libraries in the United States (ALA, 2008). For many families, the library is the primary source for pre-literacy education for children and English classes for adults. Libraries can meet the literacy needs of the community by offering Family Literacy Storytime programs.

STORYTIME CAN PROVIDE LANGUAGE LEARNING ENVIRONMENT

By offering a literacy storytime, families are reached before children go to school. Traditional library storytimes provide infants through kindergarten-age children a fun-filled learning environment that helps them build pre-literacy and social skills. With an adjustment in focus, the storytime environment can provide a language learning environment for the parents as well. When libraries offer a program that meets the needs of preschool *and* adult learners, both parents and children begin acquiring skills that can make a big difference for their future success in school and at work. The Family Literacy Storytime provides the environment for families to build these skills.

ADULTS AND CHILDREN PRACTICE LANGUAGE SKILLS

Libraries open their doors and provide a welcoming and safe place for families who are new to the English language. They are a source of information about the community, and offer resources for employment and provide community gathering space. Family Literacy Storytimes can support the new English learners by offering a small and friendly group setting for learning to communicate in English. This connection to the community can be a place for friendships to form. The format of Family Literacy Storytime helps both adults and children increase their vocabulary and familiarity with English phrases and grammar. It gives them a comfortable place to practice their new language skills in a playful, no-pressure setting.

LIBRARIES SUPPORT PARENTS

By including in library collections books in English as well as in the family's first language, libraries encourage parents to read aloud to their children. This alone makes a huge difference in the success for the child. According to Weigel and colleagues, "A child between ages one and six who shares a book with an adult for 15 minutes a day will have had 455 hours of individual reading instruction before entering school" (Weigel, Behal, and Martin, 2001). Storytime can help parents develop the habit of reading to their children each day. The storytime is an informal learning environment that fosters learning in a natural way. It includes plenty of laughter and fun, which makes the experience memorable. Although the storyteller adjusts the material presented to the level of the participants, there are no tests or textbooks to cause anxiety. Learning occurs at a pace that is right for each individual.

The Family Literacy Storytime also provides a model for oral fluency and read-aloud skills. The storyteller's use of conversational English allows both the child and the parent to develop an ear for English grammar and vocabulary. The opening activities and conversations between books, the stories told, and the questions asked all provide exposure to English at an appropriate level of difficulty. The repetition that is built into storytimes is very important for acquiring a language. When the storyteller reads books he or she demonstrates skills for the parents that will help them in reading aloud at home. By example we encourage the use of voice inflection, pacing the story, pointing to letters and pictures, retelling, and asking the children to predict. Parents learn rhymes and songs at storytime that they can repeat with their child. They also receive take-home activities including crafts, recipes, coloring pages, and finger puppets. Patterns for visual aids such as stick puppets or flannel board figures give parents and children a chance to retell stories at home, which will reinforce vocabulary and help to develop narrative skill. Play-based learning activities have been proven successful to foster academic and attention skills for preschool children (Duncan et al., 2007).

LIBRARIES SELECT APPROPRIATE BOOKS

Selecting appropriate books for reading aloud to young children requires experience and skill. Attendance at Family Literacy Storytime provides parents with exposure to a variety of age-appropriate literature. Many times families want to check out the books that were read at storytime. In addition to these, the storyteller may choose to display additional age-appropriate books that may be checked out. Included among these can be books that work well for a large group, as well as books that are best shared one on one. If possible, books in the first language of the families that attend storytime should also be displayed. Hearing books read aloud in both languages will help the child become fully bilingual. When parents read aloud in their first language they read with confidence and their love for the story will certainly show. When parents read aloud in English they will improve fluency, improve their accent, and learn new vocabulary.

LIBRARIES HELP PARENTS AND CHILDREN SUCCEED

When parents read to children, they are helping to build pathways in their brains needed for success in reading. Listening to stories increases a child's attention span and ability to focus on what is said. Children who have many books in the home are naturally curious. Exposure to lots of books increases knowledge of the world, and for new English learners it provides insight into the culture in which they are now living.

Family Literacy Storytime can be the most important program offered at the public library because the benefits are so far reaching. By helping parents and children assimilate into their new community, acquire skills in English, and develop a love for books, the pattern is set for success in school and employment. By providing a fun-filled, low-pressure place to learn, libraries are giving a great gift to families. They are allowing families to experience the joy of books.

REFERENCES

American Library Association. 2008. "Number of Libraries in the United States" ALA Fact Sheet 1 (April, 2008). Available: www.ala.org/ (accessed June 20, 2008).

Duncan, Greg J. et al. 2007. "School Readiness and Later Achievement." Developmental Psychology 43, no. 6 (November): 1428–1446. As quoted in "Children's Early Skills Predict Later School Success." TherapyTimes.com. Available: http://therapytimes.com/content= 1002J84C4896969040A040441 (accessed September 2, 2008).

National Center for Family Literacy. 2008. "Family Literacy & You." Available: www.famlit.org/ site/c.gtJWJdMQIsE/b.1351223/k.6392/Family_Literacy__You.htm (accessed June 2, 2008).

National Institute for Early Education Research. 2007. "Access to High-Quality Pre-K Severely Limited for Children from Lower Middle-Income Families." Available: http:// nieer.org/mediacenter/index.php?PressID=76 (accessed October 21, 2008).

Weigel, Dan, Patricia Behal, and Sally Martin. 2001. "The Family Storyteller: A Collaborative Family Literacy Program." *Journal of Extension* 30, no. 4 (August 2001). Available: www.joe.org/joe/2001august/iw2.html (accessed June 2, 2008).

Chapter 2

Meeting the Needs of the Adult in Family Literacy Storytime

Adults who attend the Family Literacy Storytime may be English language learners or native English speakers who are non-readers. They may be hesitant to speak or participate at first. It is important to establish a comfortable environment where the adults are accepted and valued as their child's teacher. The challenge for the storyteller is to include the adults in the learning activities without patronizing them. By enlisting their help in teaching the songs and rhymes to the child, both the children and the adults have a good time and improve their literacy skills.

BUILD ORAL FLUENCY

One of the benefits of storytime is building oral fluency. When learning a second language it is important to hear it spoken clearly, and to hear the vocabulary repeated frequently. Storytime is an ideal setting for this kind of language practice. In this natural conversational environment, adult English language learners will expand their vocabulary and train their ear to hear English sounds. They will listen and repeat songs and rhymes, giving them the opportunity to mimic the sounds of a native English speaker, which will improve their accent and vocabulary.

Building fluency activities into the storytime will help adults improve their pronunciation and comprehension. Echo reading is a listen and repeat activity. The presenter reads a phrase and asks the participants to repeat it. This adds fun and variety to the storytime, and also provides the opportunity for language learners to mimic the inflection and pronunciation of the presenter. Choral reading is similar. Participants are asked to read a phrase together out loud. The support of reading as a group gives shy readers more confidence.

IMPROVE SKILLS FOR ADULT NON-READERS

Storytime is an ideal setting for improving reading skills for adult non-readers. Parents who attend storytime with their child will become more familiar with phonics and expand the words they recognize by sight. As they help their child, parents will naturally improve their own literacy. The goal will be for them to become comfortable reading aloud to their child. By guiding parents to books with large fonts, not too much text on the page, and plenty of repetition, they can experience success. The child will know that the parent is enjoying the experience. This is beneficial for both of them.

Vocabulary is the basis for independent reading and is important to literacy development. The presenter can help the storytime participants to learn the meaning of new words by using some simple techniques. Pre-teaching unfamiliar words before reading a book will help both adults and children to understand and remember the meaning of the words. The presenter should provide multiple exposures to words used in familiar, real-life settings. Asking questions and guiding a conversation after reading a book gives participants a chance to form sentences using the new vocabulary. It also helps to talk about words that sound alike but have different meanings (homophones) and words that look alike but have different meanings (homographs). These vocabulary activities should be repeated frequently. It takes many exposures to new vocabulary words before the word is really well understood.

Another component of comprehension is story structure. After reading a book, leading group conversations about the main characters, the setting of the story, and the events of the story will help to solidify some possibly fuzzy comprehension. Help the participants learn how to predict what will occur by looking for clues and guessing. It is helpful to pause while reading a book to allow some predicting from the group before turning the page.

IMPROVE WRITTEN ENGLISH SKILLS

In addition to oral fluency, some of the adults may be ready to improve their written English skills. This can be included in several ways. Use the white board in extended learning activities to make lists or write patterned sentences. Include a craft from time to time, and ask the children to write their names on the craft. As parents help with these activities their own writing improves. Another option is to include journals for the adults. They can write about any topic and turn in their journals after storytime. The storyteller responds and returns the journal the following week, ending with a question that will motivate the writer to respond in the next entry. These individual private conversations in writing will build confidence and help the adults find their voice. The storyteller models correct writing, guides the writer with questions or comments, and rewards the writer with praise for his efforts. Clarena Lorrotta, an ESL instructor in Texas, found that journaling provided her students the opportunity to experiment with the written form of language in a non-threatening way (Lorrotta, 2008).

ENCOURAGE INDEPENDENT PRACTICE

Independent practice is important for language learners. Storytime occurs just once a week; when providing handouts and patterns (to take home) families will be more likely to practice on their own. Teach the participants how to use a dictionary so they can add to their vocabulary during the normal course of their days. Encourage families to check out library books to take home, and when possible give them books to keep. With plenty of exposure to both written and spoken language and natural and fun ways to explore it, the participants will make great strides in learning English.

REFERENCE

Lorrotta, Clarena. 2008. "Written Conversations with Hispanic Adults Developing English Literacy." *Adult Basic Education and Literacy Journal* 2, no. 3 (Spring): 22.

Chapter 3

Meeting the Needs of the Child in Family Literacy Storytime

Most children who attend Family Literacy Storytimes are learning English as a second language while they are still developing comprehension in their first language. At first they may be shy. They may not answer questions. They may not participate in the songs and fingerplays. With patience and gentle coaxing and plenty of modeling the actions for the songs and rhymes, the children will slowly become comfortable and their participation will increase.

STORYTIME EXPERIENCE BUILDS COMPREHENSION

The Family Literacy Storytime experience can build English comprehension for children through repetition, conversation, and questions. Choose a few songs and rhymes to repeat almost every week so the children can feel confident about them. Speak slowly and clearly but with normal inflection so the child begins to develop an ear for English. Ask questions in patterns, repeating a common phrase each time. Choose books that are your favorites, and if you get a good response from the children read those books frequently.

OLDER SIBLINGS HELP YOUNGER CHILDREN

It is a challenge to prepare and present a storytime for a wide age range. Bring several books with you, even though you may only read two. This gives you flexibility to read the book that meets the needs of the group that comes to storytime that day. Invite older siblings to help younger children with the fingerplays or rhymes. They can be very valuable helpers and they will feel important. When you choose to read a book for younger children, you can introduce it by asking the older children, "Was this one of your favorite books when you were little? It is one of my favorites, too."

DEVELOPMENTAL STAGES IN ACQUIRING EARLY LITERACY SKILLS

The Child Language and Early Literacy Skill Development chart (p. 10) explains the general developmental stages children follow in acquiring early literacy skills.

It is helpful to know, for example, that a child does not understand the difference between real and make believe until about age five. When you understand this, you know that folktales are best for ages five and up. The younger children will understand a book about shopping for shoes or going to the park much better. A three-year-old can follow directions given one at a time. You may be in a habit of addressing children like this. "Come in! Put your coat over there. Have a seat." Be careful about giving too many directions at once to avoid confusing the children. During the first five years the brain develops critical pathways for learning. Introduce music and rhythm, counting, colors, small and large motor skills and lots of vocabulary at storytimes to stimulate these brain pathways.

Child Language and Early Literacy Skill Development

Babies

Use gestures to communicate

Distinguish emotion by the tone of voice

Babble with inflection

Very skilled at hearing differences in sounds

Brain is developing critical pathways

Brain doubles in size in first year

Likes to hold, chew, and throw books

One Year

Can understand much more language than can say

Can say 5 to 50 words

Enjoy repetitive and predictable books

Can turn pages

Prefer illustrations with lots of white space and simple shapes

Two Years

Vocabulary of 50 to 200 words

Learns the meaning of eight new words a day

Forms short sentences

Short attention span

Prefer books about their own experiences

Can count a few objects

Enjoys clapping and fingerplay rhymes

Three Years

Vocabulary of 900 words

Wants to hear favorite stories repeated

Can follow directions given one at a time

Can talk about books and answer questions

Four Years

Vocabulary of 1,500 words

Can form complete sentences

Grammatical skills develop (verb endings, plurals, connecting words)

Understands time, seasons

Can follow two unrelated directions

Five Years

Vocabulary of 3,000 words

Good attention span

Understands the difference between real and make believe

Knows that a story has a beginning, middle, and end

Can create and tell a story

Want to know more about child development and pre-literacy skills?

See these Web sites:

www.growupreading.org
www.cdipage.com
www.learningpt.org/pdfs/literacy/readingbirthtofive.pdf

PRE-LITERACY SKILLS

The Public Library Association has identified six pre-literacy skills. Storytime is a perfect place to introduce these skills to children and their parents. They are: vocabulary, print awareness, print motivation, letter knowledge, narrative skill, and phonological awareness. By including games that provide fun and activities focused on these skills children begin to associate the library and reading with a pleasant experience. The Family Literacy Storytime plans incorporate these six pre-literacy skills into each program. Over time, children can develop strength in all six skills through storytime participation.

MULTI-SENSORY EXPERIENCES

Multi-sensory experiences delight the young child. Provide board books with touch and feel pages. Use rhythm instruments with the children and include dancing or marching as a rest activity between books. Bring real objects (hats, shoes, toys, tools, live animals) to introduce the storytime theme. Occasionally include food to taste at storytime, such as making butter from cream by shaking it in a jar. Collect a variety of craft materials to give children experience with coloring and pasting. Provide threading beads, wooden puzzles and lacing boards to help children develop motor skills.

Young children have a short attention span. You can hold their attention throughout the storytime by including play in your plans. Rest activities such as clapping rhymes, action rhymes and fingerplays give children a chance to move their bodies between books. Reward children with play after you have finished reading books. Easy games can be planned for the end of storytime, such as Ring Around the Rosie or Duck Duck Goose. Children will enjoy manipulating flannel board objects that you used for a story. Making storytime a structured playtime will help children stay focused longer.

ALTERNATE STORY FORMATS

Stories may be presented in a variety of formats. In addition to books, each storytime should include an alternate format story. Flannel or magnet boards, hand puppets, stick puppets and flash cards add variety. They also help the child develop an ear for English and for the pattern of story. Don't hesitate to allow the children to handle these visual aids after you have told the story. Helping children retell the story using these visual aids develops narrative skills.

CREATING A STORYTIME SPACE

Creating a storytime space is a kind of signature piece that each storyteller develops (for tips, see p. 12). Setting the stage for storytime helps the children settle down and recognize that this is quiet time. Changing the appearance of the room sends a signal that what is about to happen is special. Children will begin to modify their behavior during storytime. They will come to expect singing, books, rhymes, stories and fingerplays. They will develop the ability to focus and participate.

Creating a Storytime Space

Set out a carpet square for each child.
Use a storytime rug or quilt on the floor.
Play music as children are entering the room.
Use the same puppet to welcome the children each time.
Develop a welcome ritual, such as "high 5" or handshakes.
Form a circle holding hands, say a rhyme together, and then sit down.

Chapter 4

Combining Pre-reading Skills for Children with Literacy Skills for the Adult

Family Literacy Storytime provides the setting to combine learning activities with family fun. It is a venue for offering pre-reading skills for children simultaneously with language and literacy skills for the adults. For this to be successful, both children and adults must be welcomed and respected.

The adults at Family Literacy Storytime may be well-educated non-native English speakers. They may feel awkward communicating in English, and frustrated that they cannot express themselves as fluently as they do in their first language. They want to have the respect of their child, so they may hesitate to answer questions in English and show their incompetence. Other adults at Family Literacy Storytime may be native English speakers with low reading skills. They may hesitate to read aloud or join in the rhymes and games. The storyteller must therefore use diplomacy, patience, and tact to encourage the adults to participate. Genuine praise and respect should help the adults to feel comfortable. Whatever reading skills or English competency the adult has represents a good effort on their part, and each achievement is a milestone.

PARENT AND CHILD HAVE FUN AT STORYTIME

A primary motivation for parents to bring their children to Family Literacy Storytime is having fun with their child. The storytime programs should include lots of time for the parent and child to cuddle and tickle, play clapping games, and create crafts. This gives them experiences to talk about, which is good for oral fluency. It gives them a positive library experience. Parents feel good about providing this enjoyable opportunity by bringing their child to the library. Both parents and children associate reading together with having fun, which will have a positive impact on the number of hours they spend reading together at home.

PARENTS RECEIVE MATERIALS TO USE AT HOME

Learning new vocabulary can be a shared experience if families are given a picture dictionary to use at home. With grant funds it may be possible for each family that registers for Family Literacy Storytime to receive a dictionary. If this is part of your library's program, include a dictionary moment in each storytime. Take note of an unfamiliar word as you read a book.

Then look up the word in the picture dictionary. This modeling will encourage families to look up words at home.

Give parents a copy or pattern for the visual aids that you use at storytime and encourage them to repeat the rhyme or story at home. Children love repetition and will ask for favorites again and again. If the parents have these tools readily available it will be easy for them to extend the learning experience beyond storytime. Over time, they can build a nice collection of visual aids for use at home. Be sure to offer another copy of a handout from previous weeks to replace their worn-out copy. How wonderful that their stick puppets were so well loved that they became tattered!

STEPS IN LANGUAGE DEVELOPMENT

The steps in language development for a second language apply to adults and children. Becoming aware of these steps (see below) will help the storyteller understand the response (or non-response) of the participants. Gentle coaxing and patience will go far to encourage them to try out their new language skills. Repetition, speaking slowly, and careful pronunciation on the part of the storyteller will help the participants understand and develop the skills to reply in the new language. Using gestures and giving other non-verbal clues will help participants understand. Using manipulatives will give participants a chance to repeat the story and reinforce new vocabulary. Routines are important, because participants will soon know what to expect. Including a running commentary about what you are doing provides more language exposure and increases understanding.

Steps in Language Development

Absorbing
Understanding is limited. Unable to respond in second language.

Gesturing
Body language and facial expressions as well as gestures compose most of the communication.

Spectating
Watching other members of the group to see what works.

Rehearsing
Saying rhymes and singing songs over and over to experience success with the second language, both silently and orally.

Mimicking
Acquiring the ability to produce sounds in second language. Developing an ear for the sounds of second language and minimizing noticeable accent.

Communicating
Confidence is sufficient to respond and ask questions in the second language.

FURTHER READING

All of the following articles are available from EBSCOhost.

Jackson, Young C., and Helen Bell. 2008. "Learning Side by Side." *American Libraries* 39, no. 4 (April): 68–69.

Ma, James. 2008. "Reading the Word and the World"—How Mind and Culture Are Mediated through the Use of Dual-language Storybooks. *Education 3-13* 36, no. 3 (August): 237–251.

Mui, Selina, and Jim Anderson. 2008. "At Home with the Johars: Another Look at Family Literacy." *Reading Teacher* 62, no. 3 (November): 234–243.

Saracho, Olivia N. 2008. "A Literacy Program for Fathers: A Case Study." *Early Childhood Education Journal* 35, no. 4 (February): 351–356.

St. Clair, Ralf. 2008. "Reading, Writing, and Relationships: Human and Social Capital in Family Literacy Programs." *Adult Basic Education and Literacy* 2, no. 2 (Summer): 84–93.

Chapter 5

Storytime Basics

Planning and presenting a storytime is a skill that is developed over time. Each storyteller has a unique style. Some basic ideas for storytime planning that have been successful for others may be helpful for storytellers who are starting Family Literacy Storytimes in their library.

CONSISTENT ENVIRONMENT

Create a storytime space that is consistent week to week (see Chapter 3). Change the room visually by placing a rug, blanket, or carpet squares on the floor. This sets the space apart and gives a subliminal message to the children that will help them prepare mentally for storytime. Some storytellers like to play a CD of background music, children's songs or nature sounds to welcome participants to the storytime space. It is an auditory clue that storytime is beginning.

CONSISTENT FORMAT

Use a standard opening and closing song or rhyme (see, e.g., "Goodbye for Now," p. 38, and "Time for Storytime," p. 47). Familiarity is comforting. Hearing the same song each week as storytime opens sends a signal that the program is beginning. Children know what is expected of them. The opening and closing songs often become favorites that children will sing during playtime because they know these songs well. Storytellers sometimes use the same songs for a year, and then select a new opening and closing for the following year. Other storytellers use the same opening and closing for many years. On the *Mr. Rogers* television program, you may recall, the same song was sung at the beginning of his show. This is personal preference.

VISUAL AIDS

Use visual aids, puppets, toys, and real objects from home to introduce your storytime theme. The more senses that are engaged, the more memorable the experience will be. Bring in household items to display. Your kitchen bowls, photos, music boxes, or hats will be intriguing. Children will enjoy seeing a story illustrated with flannel or magnet board figures and will happily retell the story later using those pieces. Puppets can be hugged and petted by the children. Some children will enjoy this and others may be a little afraid of the puppets, so always make it optional. The toy or puppet may be able to gently soothe a child who is crying.

BUILD A FOUNDATION WITH SONGS AND RHYMES

Build a repertoire of songs, nursery rhymes and rhyming stories by repeating them frequently, and slowly adding new material (see Chapters 9 ,10, and 11). Over time, the children and their parents will learn many rhymes well. These become the foundation of their new language. The sentence patterns and vocabulary they learn will help them create sentences independently. Rhythm and rhyme are powerful memory aids for both adults and children. Rhythm skills form a foundation for math and music skills as children grow. Singing a song between books gives children a rest from sitting still, and provides a chance for movement. This adds to the fun, but also is necessary for development of motor skills.

SELECT APPROPRIATE BOOKS

Select books with large clear illustrations and generous white space. Young children have not developed vision enough to focus on dark or detailed artwork. Books with repetitive text naturally invite children to join in. A cumulative story has a pattern that is soon recognized. When children know what is coming next in the story it gives them a feeling of success and power. They will happily repeat the refrain. Funny books are almost always successful. Humor is different from culture to culture, but the humor in most children's books is gentle and universally accepted. Because of your culturally diverse group, select books that include positive cultural images and ethnic diversity. Retellings of traditional stories are also a good choice for children who are old enough to understand them. They may be too long and too complex for toddlers.

LITERACY FOCUS

Plan connecting activities with a literacy focus. Each storytime should focus on just one of the six pre-literacy skills. Over time, the children will be introduced to all six. This will simplify planning for the storyteller. Parents and children will be more likely to internalize the concept of the day, also.

Include vocabulary-building games. For example, say "I am thinking of something blue." Invite participants to guess what you are thinking. Ask children to name something that they are wearing. Ask them to tell the group what they ate for breakfast.

Provide opportunities for children to retell a story using props or flannel/magnetic board figures (see Chapter 11). Once they have heard you tell it, they will enjoy visiting the story again by putting up the figures while you narrate. Soon they will be narrating independently.

Give families flannel board figures, puppets, books, and handouts to encourage them to replay the storytime activities at home. Providing these materials will give parents a chance to talk to their children about the storytime experience. It gives the families repeated experiences with the vocabulary and literacy skill they learned at storytime. They will be more willing to join in the next time that story, song, or rhyme is presented at your storytime.

Chapter 6

Including the Six Pre-literacy Skills at Family Literacy Storytime

Each storytime program should focus on one of the six pre-literacy skills. Over time, the children will become proficient in all six. Modeling for parents is an important part of the storyteller's mandate. Providing a fun learning experience that can be repeated at home will help to extend the storytime experience. Language skills develop best when practiced frequently. Both parent and child will benefit from literacy activities that they can repeat at home.

VOCABULARY BUILDING

Repetition is very important in increasing vocabulary. Preparing storytimes based on a theme will help to ensure that vocabulary words are repeated several times in the session. For example, if the storytime theme is dogs, some core words likely to be repeated in several books and rhymes may be food, walk, dig, bark, pet, play, ball, sit. The storyteller can select core words such as these and point them out in all the books of the day and in the songs and rhymes that are included. This focus will help the participants to understand the meaning and also to retain the new words in memory.

Making storytimes memorable experiences will help the participants to truly acquire new vocabulary words. Laughing and playing together will create positive associations with reading and learning to speak English. Using props, toys and a variety of activities keeps the participants engaged and will help them make the most of the learning experience. Using flash cards, wooden blocks with letters and pictures on them, and toys or puzzles that coordinate with the books will help to make storytime fun and memorable.

Learning vocabulary through multi-sensory experiences is more successful than relying on auditory experiences alone. Include items that can be touched such as soft toy animals, real tools or household items, and board books with texture. Include video books online from time to time. Play recorded music and encourage children to dance or move with the music. Provide food once in awhile. Allow children to use modeling clay to form an image of that day's subject. Include craft projects at the end of the storytime, which serves as a take-home reminder of the vocabulary learned that day.

PHONOLOGICAL AWARENESS

Phonological awareness is hearing the sounds of language and understanding that language can be divided into parts: sentences, words, and syllables. The ability to hear when one word ends and the next begins is sophisticated. Even in the first language, this skill takes some time to develop. A second language uses some different sounds, which may be hard to hear and hard to pronounce at first. Storytime activities that develop phonological awareness include rhyme and alliteration. Rhyming songs help children substitute a different initial sound of a word while keeping the same ending sound. Alliteration books include a number of words that begin with the same sound. The storyteller can draw attention to these sounds as the book is read or the songs are sung. Clapping while saying a nursery rhyme can help children hear the syllables of the words. It also adds to the fun because it includes movement.

LETTER KNOWLEDGE

Phonics is the association of symbols or letters with the sounds of language. Storytellers can help children understand the sounds associated with letters by pointing to letters and saying the sound. Children can be encouraged to repeat the sound. They will enjoy identifying the letters and sounds of their name. They will enjoy the game of looking for the "B" on a page of the book you are reading. Drawing a letter in the air with their fingers, children can begin to visualize the shapes of letters. By talking slowly and pointing to the written letters on a flash card or on the white board while sounding out a well-known word, the storyteller can help children hear the segments of a word. A puppet can sound out a word while the children cheer him on. The puppet can also remove the first sound of a word, and the children will enjoy guessing the word. For example, book becomes "ook." Chair becomes "air." Then a new beginning sound can be added. "Ook" becomes Look. "Air" becomes Fair.

Playing with magnetic letters can help children become familiar with the shapes of the letters. The storyteller can draw letters on the white board. Children can trace letters on a textured surface such as a carpet square or sandpaper. Craft activities can include writing their name, or coloring the shape of a letter and a picture of an object that begins with that letter sound. Engaging many senses enhances the learning experience.

PRINT MOTIVATION

Print motivation is being interested in and enjoying books. Very young children need to handle board books so they can learn to turn the pages and look at the pictures. The storyteller should select books for storytime that she enjoys. The enthusiasm that the storyteller shows for the books will help the children to enjoy them. Children should see parents and other adults reading and talking about books. The most colorful, fun, and excellent children's literature should be propped on the table at storytime. Families should be encouraged to take them home. If the home is filled with books, children will fall in love with books.

The atmosphere of the storytime should be fun with very little demand for the children to sit still and listen. Inviting the child with a pleasant voice, using lots of inflection while reading, and animated talking about the books will help to create positive associations with storytime. Beautiful pop-up books, or books about interesting subjects such as dinosaurs and trucks, can grab the curiosity of the child. If the best books are introduced at storytime, and the storyteller genuinely loves them, the children will be motivated too.

PRINT AWARENESS

Children with print awareness understand that letters and words on the page are the source of the story or the information. They understand that when someone reads a book the reader is reading the words, not the pictures on the page. Print awareness is knowing that print has different functions such as telling a story or giving directions. As children develop print awareness they will notice print on road signs, exit signs, on the sides of buildings, on menus and on buses and taxis.

By pointing to the print and moving the finger across the page the storyteller can help children realize that in English books are read from left to right. Children can be encouraged to wave to the left and wave to the right because that is the direction for reading. The storyteller can also draw attention to the print in the books. Before reading, show and talk about the title on the cover. If the word "dog" appears on the cover, show "dog" again when it appears in the text of the book. This will help children to realize that text sizes and font styles may differ but the word is the same.

NARRATIVE SKILL

Narrative skill is the ability to describe events with expressive language, retell an experience, and repeat the events of a story in order. Conversation after reading a book is an important part of Family Literacy Storytimes. Talking to children with expressive language enhances narrative skill. Asking open-ended questions encourages children to put their thoughts into words. Repeat the child's words, then ask a follow-up question. This lets the child know he was understood and it encourages dialogue. Modeling oral fluency and question techniques will help both parents and children in the Family Literacy Storytime. It gives them English language patterns that they adopt and customize. It helps parents develop the skills of asking questions and repeating the child's answer. It helps parents learn to guide their child in describing events and telling stories.

After reading a story, the storyteller can provide visual aids that will help the group retell the story. Toys, hand puppets, finger puppets, or flannel board figures can be used to prompt their memory. After storytime, a parent and child may want to revisit the story and retell it with or without props. Planning time for this activity after storytime is important. With practice, narrative skills improve. This builds the children's confidence that they can express themselves in the second language effectively. Narrative skill in preschool children is a good predictor of reading success in school. Parents who learn to ask open-ended questions and guide their children in retelling stories will help them acquire fluency in spoken English. Of course, the parent's skill with English is also growing. At the same time, their children are preparing to become fluent readers.

Chapter 7

National, State, and Local Organizations That Support Family Literacy

Many resources are available for librarians who are interested in literacy. The following list of selected resources can provide model programs, ideas for printed handouts, and networking possibilities. National organizations have the resources to fund research, which can be meaningful to those who are beginning a literacy project. State and local agencies may be able to provide materials and resources that are more targeted to the local population.

NATIONAL CENTER FOR FAMILY LITERACY

www.famlit.org

Read articles about national family literacy success stories and programs. Find a local literacy program by clicking on the United States map. Read the Literacy Now blog. Read about the National Conference on Family Literacy.

Quotes from this Web site:

- Parental literacy is one of the single most important indicators of a child's success. The National Assessment of Education Progress (NAEP) has concluded that youngsters whose parents are functionally illiterate are twice as likely to be functionally illiterate themselves.
- By age four, children who live in poor families will have heard 32 *million* fewer words than children living in professional families.

Family literacy teaches families that they can learn together, that learning is a mutual process, that learning is fun, and—significantly—that education has a beneficial social impact as well as a financial one.

All parents want their children to succeed, and all parents have valuable experiences that can help their children succeed. By incorporating strategies for supporting children's literacy development in the educational experiences of adults, family literacy makes parent involvement more effective and meaningful.

Many different types of programs incorporate family literacy strategies, from summer reading programs in libraries to community youth programs to elementary schools to job-preparation programs. With its focus on the family as a catalyst for change, family literacy forges an educational bond between parent and child that will last for generations.

THE BARBARA BUSH FOUNDATION FOR FAMILY LITERACY

www.barbarabushfoundation.com

This Web site provides information about grants that are available to support literacy programs. Annual fund-raisers are hosted by the Bush family and feature readings from best-selling authors. An article reports lessons learned from the nearly 700 family literacy programs supported by the Barbara Bush foundation.

Quotes from this Web site:

- The instructional design of many effective family literacy programs includes four integrated components: literacy instruction for parents, pre-reading activities for children, parent and child together time, and parent group time.
- Parents often enjoy reading children's books to their young children. The activity has a multiple impact. Parents who may be reluctant to read "out loud" if other adults can hear them feel comfortable reading to a young child. The activity creates a bond between parent and child, and the child learns that reading is an important activity.

NATIONAL INSTITUTE FOR LITERACY

www.nifl.gov

The National Institute for Literacy, a federal agency, provides leadership on literacy issues, including the improvement of reading instruction for children, youths, and adults. Fact sheets are based on scientific research. Publications can be requested and will be sent free of charge. *Catalyst* is the institution's new quarterly newsletter.

Quote from this Web site:

- In consultation with the U.S. Departments of Education, Labor, and Health and Human Services, the Institute serves as a national resource on current, comprehensive literacy research, practice, and policy. The institute is authorized under the No Child Left Behind (NCLB) law to help children, youths, and adults learn to read by supporting and disseminating scientifically based reading research.

Publications include:

Literacy Begins at Home: Teach Them to Read
Shining Stars—Toddlers Get Ready to Read
Shining Stars—Preschoolers Get Ready to Read
A Child Becomes A Reader
Put Reading First

NATIONAL EVEN START ASSOCIATION

www.evenstart.org/

Even Start Family Literacy Programs are school-community partnerships that help break the cycle of poverty and illiteracy by integrating early childhood education, adult literacy or adult basic education, and parenting education into a unified family literacy program.

COLORIN COLORADO

www.colorincolorado.org

Colorin Colorado has articles, resources and ideas for parents and teachers of English language learners. The focus is children including babies, toddlers, and students pre-K through grade 12. This resource includes research-based reports, toolkits, podcasts, and book reviews. Although the primary focus of this Web site is for Spanish speakers, there are resources in other languages also (Arabic, Chinese, Haitian Creole, Hmong, Korean, Navajo, Russian, Tagalog, Vietnamese).

ENGLISH AS A SECOND LANGUAGE IN THE USA

www.eslinusa.com/

This organization provides information about private programs for adult learners of English as a Second Language. The Web site includes a directory of ESL programs and schools by state.

U.S.A. LEARNS!

www.usalearns.org/

U.S.A. Learns! helps adults get basic skills to help them succeed as workers, family members, and citizens. The major areas of support are Adult Basic Education, Adult Secondary Education, and English Language Acquisition. These programs emphasize basic skills such as reading, writing, math, English language competency and problem solving. It is developed by the U.S. Department of Education and the California Department of Education. Online courses are available in three levels: beginning, low intermediate, and intermediate. Users must register to access the courses.

THE ROLE OF LIBRARIANS IN LITERACY EDUCATION

www.libraryinstruction.com/literacy-education.html

This Web site provides information about ways that public libraries serve as an educational agency as lifelong learning centers. Public libraries are serving adults, teens, and children with tutors, classes, and programs tailored to meet the needs of their surrounding communities.

BORN LEARNING

www.bornlearning.org

Born Learning is a public awareness campaign sponsored by United Way of America, to raise public awareness of family literacy needs. It provides television, radio, and print ads and public service announcements designed to turn everyday moments into teaching opportunities. This organization offers information and printable resources for parents, grandparents, and caregivers of young children.

AMERICA'S LITERACY DIRECTORY

www.literacydirectory.org

A service of the National Institute for Literacy, this directory connects tutors with both adult learners and children who want help with reading and writing, want to improve math skills, or need help learning English as a second language.

STATE LIBRARIES (SELECTED EXAMPLES)

State libraries offer a variety of literacy resources. From your state's library Web site, you can find local literacy programs that meet the needs of adult learners as well as preschool children and students. A few examples follow.

California Library Literacy Services
http://libraryliteracy.org

Find out how to become a volunteer, get help with your reading, find literacy services for adults or families, or participate in adult learners' writing contests.

Massachusetts Board of Library Commissioners
http://mblc.state.ma.us/libraries/literacy/index.php

Provides a directory of services provided by Massachusetts libraries, and links to online literacy resources.

Quote from this Web site:

- Library-based literacy services provide basic skills instruction to adults with low literacy skills. These programs support the library's mission as a center for life-long learning. Individual programs vary from one library to the next. Many programs utilize trained volunteers who provide basic literacy training through one-on-one tutoring, whereas others offer small group instruction.

Missouri State Library Literacy Services

www.sos.mo.gov/library/development/literacy

The Web site provides information about library literacy programs, conferences, and workshops that support literacy services, and information about grants available to support family literacy programs.

Quote from this Web site:

- A number of libraries provide ESOL (English for Speakers of Other Languages) services for persons with limited English proficiency. The library may also offer special services such as family literacy which targets whole families for learning, citizenship preparation or training for the GED or the High School equivalency exam.

Nevada State Literacy Resource Center

http://nevadaculture.org/docs/nsla/lpd/literacy

The Nevada State Literacy Resource Center (SLRC) supports state, county, and local literacy programs. It provides a collection of books and media for literacy instruction and programs for literacy students, trainers and tutors.

Colorado Libraries for Early Literacy (CLEL)

www.clel.org

A Colorado Department of Education initiative, CLEL provides literacy service to children, parents, child care providers, and library staff.

Quote from this Web site:

- An important way to reach the 45% of young children who do NOT attend licensed childcare, along with their parents and caregivers, is through public library programs, collections and services.

COMMUNITY COLLEGE ESL PROGRAMS

www.eslinusa.com/esl_at_community_colleges.html

This is a Web directory of ESL programs at United States community colleges. Programs are both credited and non-credited. Some offer individual tutors. The classes are designed to help immigrant students develop listening and writing skills in English. Includes ESL programs and schools in the following states:

California	Maryland	Ohio
Colorado	Massachusetts	Texas
Illinois	Minnesota	Washington
Indiana	Nebraska	
Kansas	New York	

PART II

FAMILY LITERACY STORYTIME PROGRAMS

Chapter 8

Family Literacy Storytime Planning Ideas

Planning your family literacy storytime will give you a road map to follow when you are in front of the group. Using the Family Literacy Storytime Planning Form (p. 32) will help you remember what you used and the date of your presentation. These planning forms can be helpful from year to year. When you repeat this theme next time, by making just a few changes and adding one or two new books, your storytime is already planned.

Choose your standard opening and closing activity. A song or action rhyme that you enjoy is best, because you will be using it for a long time. Some storytellers choose a new opening and closing activity each year. Others stick with the one they know and love year after year.

Select a theme for your storytime. A theme is not as important to the participants as it is to the presenter, but a theme helps you focus your book and activity selection. You may start with themes based on the seasons, local events, and holidays. You may build a whole program based on a new book that really appeals to you, adding other familiar books and activities that are related in some way. You may choose a concept for your theme, such as counting or colors. This book contains 25 storytime themes with ready-to-use plans (see Chapter 12).

Choose one of the six pre-literacy skills as your focus for the day. This narrow focus will ensure that the participants get plenty of repetition, which will aid in comprehension. Over time, you will acquaint the storytime families with all six pre-literacy skills.

Choose at least four books for your storytime. Having more than enough material at hand gives you flexibility when you are in front of the group. Whether you have mostly toddlers or kindergarteners you are prepared with a few books that are just right for them.

Think about the extended learning activities that you can include based on the books you have selected. Make a few notes for yourself and collect any additional materials you may need, such as a white board and markers or puppets.

Select a few nursery rhymes, songs or action rhymes. It is a good idea to repeat these week after week, slowly adding new activities. Repeat familiar rhymes that you have not used for a few weeks so the storytime families will remember them. Revisiting favorites will usually elicit smiles and enthusiasm from the children.

Prepare the handouts or craft activities. Give families copies of the visual aids that you use in storytime so they can repeat these activities at home. Repetition is the best way to acquire new vocabulary. As families repeat storytime games and rhymes, they will talk to one another and laugh together. This positive reinforcement goes a long way in building pre-literacy skills and fluency in the new language.

Family Literacy Storytime Planning Form

Theme: _____

Presentation dates: _____

Literacy skill focus: _____

Books:

_____
_____
_____
_____

Extended learning activities:

_____
_____
_____
_____

Songs, rhymes and rhyming stories:

_____
_____
_____
_____

Handouts, crafts, or patterns:

_____
_____
_____
_____

Notes:

_____
_____
_____
_____

Number of participants: _____

Ages of the children: _____

Collect books to prop up that are available to check out. You can select books based on the storytime theme. Be sure to also include new books, pop-up books, recipe books, or craft books that you think will be of interest to your group.

After you complete your storytime, make notes on your planning form to remind you of the favorite activities and the response of the group. Make notes of books that did not work well because the vocabulary was too difficult or the pictures were too small. You may also want to note the number of participants and the ages of the children for your records and future planning.

Chapter 9

Music for Family Literacy Storytimes

Music is the universal language. You will find that children will respond to music by moving! Dancing or clapping or nodding with the rhythm of the song is a natural response. Learning and memory are enhanced when melody is included, so singing is an easy way to learn and remember new vocabulary.

Starting and ending your storytime with a song provides structure for your program. Repeating songs frequently helps both children and adults to learn them. Once they know the songs well, repeating them brings a smile to their faces.

Draw upon your favorite children's songs as you plan your storytimes. If you enjoy the songs, your enthusiasm will naturally transfer to your storytime group. This chapter also provides new original songs that encourage movement, teach a concept or celebrate everyday pleasures. As you learn the songs and teach them to your regular storytime children and parents, new favorites are sure to emerge.

Colors

Kathryn Totten

Family

Kathryn Totten

Goodbye for Now

Kathryn Totten

Leaves Are Falling

Kathryn Totten

Letters

Kathryn Totten

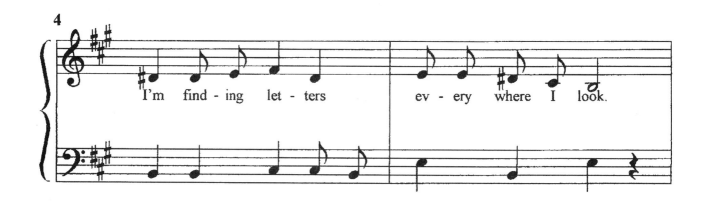

My Meals

Kathryn Totten

Pizza Popcorn Peanuts

Kathryn Totten

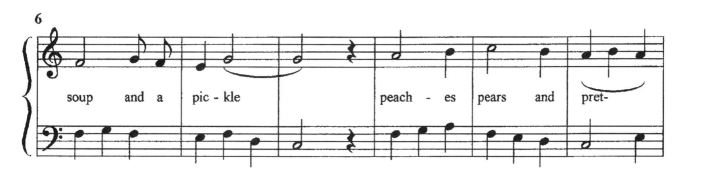

Raise Them High

Kathryn Totten

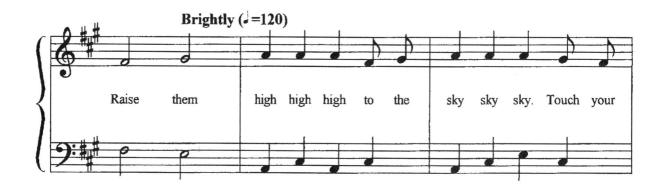

Someday I Would

Kathryn Totten

Storytime Dance

Kathryn Totten

Time for Storytime

Kathryn Totten

Cheerfully

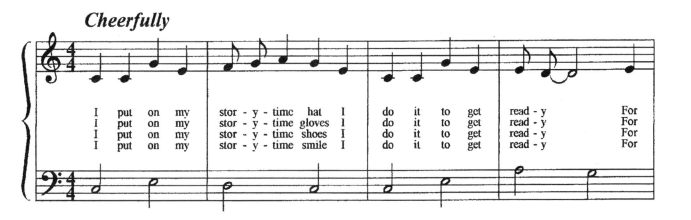

I put on my stor - y - time hat I do it to get read - y For
I put on my stor - y - time gloves I do it to get read - y For
I put on my stor - y - time shoes I do it to get read - y For
I put on my stor - y - time smile I do it to get read - y For

(4)

here I am with stor - y - time friends It's time for stor - y - time. And
here I am with stor - y - time friends. It's time for stor - y - time.
here I am with stor - y - time friends. It's time for stor - y - time.
here I am with stor - y - time friends. It's time for stor - y - time.

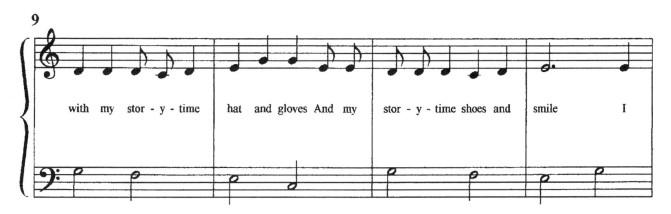

with my stor - y - time hat and gloves And my stor - y - time shoes and smile I

W Is Lots of Fun

Kathryn Totten

Would You Like to Fly?

Kathryn Totten

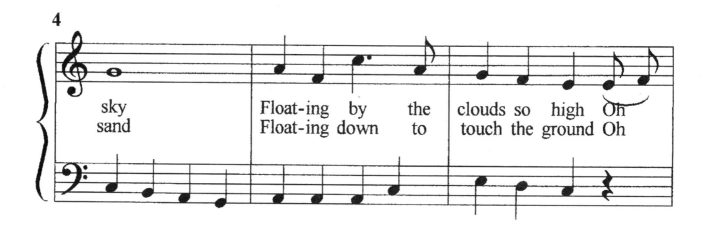

Chapter 10

Traditional Nursery Rhymes with Activities and Patterns

Every child should grow up knowing many traditional nursery rhymes. They are the building blocks of language and cultural knowledge. They are short and easy to remember, have lots of action to encourage movement, and are excellent teaching tools for the sounds of language. You don't have to select a nursery rhyme that goes with your storytime theme. Any rhyme makes a good rest activity and transition between books. You will soon learn which rhymes are favorites with your group. Since nursery rhymes are so universal, chances are the adults in your group remember a rhyme from their childhood. You may want to ask them to share a traditional rhyme in their first language.

The following rhymes are familiar and well known in the United States. After each nursery rhyme is a suggested rhyming pair to listen for, with suggested additional rhyming words. This activity can be auditory alone, or you may choose to also write the words on the white board. Soon the children will find it easy to suggest additional rhymes.

Each rhyme includes an illustration to be used on the magnet board or made into stick puppets. Some finger puppets are included as well.

Jack and Jill

Jack and Jill went up a hill
To fetch a pail of water
Jack fell down and broke his crown
And Jill came tumbling after

Listen for the rhyming words: *down* and *crown*.

More rhymes: frown, brown, town, clown.

Hickory Dickory Dock

Hickory dickory dock
The mouse ran up the clock
The clock struck one
The mouse ran down
Hickory dickory dock

Listen for the rhyming words: *dock* and *clock*.

More rhymes: sock, lock, knock, rock.

Hey Diddle Diddle

Hey diddle diddle
The cat and the fiddle
The cow jumped over the moon.
The little dog laughed
To see such a sport
And the dish ran away with the spoon

Listen for the rhyming words: *moon* and *spoon*.

More rhymes: noon, soon, June, prune.

Jack Be Nimble

Jack be nimble
Jack be quick
Jack jump over
The candle stick

Listen for the rhyming words: *quick* and *stick*.

More rhymes: thick, brick, lick, trick.

Mary, Mary Quite Contrary

Mary, Mary quite contrary,
How does your garden grow?
With silver bells and cockle shells
And pretty maids all in a row

Listen for the rhyming words: *grow* and *row*.

More rhymes: snow, blow, go, throw.

There Was an Old Woman
Who Lived in a Shoe

There was an old woman who lived in a shoe
She had so many children, she didn't know what to do
She gave them all broth without any bread
Then kissed them all soundly and put them to bed

Listen for the rhyming words: *bread* and *bed*.

More rhymes: fed, head, red, thread.

Little Bo-Peep

Little Bo-Peep has lost her sheep
And doesn't know where to find them
Leave them alone and they'll come home
Wagging their tails behind them

Listen for the rhyming words: *Bo-Peep* and *sheep*.

More rhymes: deep, sleep, leap, steep.

Humpty Dumpty

Humpty Dumpty sat on a wall
Humpty Dumpty had a great fall
All the king's horses and all the king's men
Couldn't put Humpty together again

Listen for the rhyming words: *wall* and *fall*.

More rhymes: ball, call, mall, tall.

Pussy Cat, Pussy Cat

Pussy cat, Pussy cat, where have you been?
I've been to London to visit the queen.
Pussy cat, Pussy cat, what did you there?
I frightened the little mouse under her chair.

Listen for the rhyming words: *there* and *chair*.

More rhymes: stare, bear, wear, fair.

Little Jack Horner

Little Jack Horner sat in a corner
Eating his Christmas pie
He stuck in his thumb and pulled out a plum
And said, "What a good boy am I."

Listen for the rhyming words: *thumb* and *plum*.

More rhymes: drum, some, come, gum.

Two Little Black Birds

Two little black birds sitting on a hill
One named Jack and the other named Jill
Fly away Jack. Fly away Jill.
Come back Jack. Come back Jill.

Listen for the rhyming words: *hill* and *Jill*.

More rhymes: still, fill, thrill, pill.

Here Is the Beehive

Here is the beehive
Where are the bees?
Hidden away
Where nobody sees.
Soon you will see them
Come out of the hive
One, two, three, four, five

Listen for the rhyming words: *hive* and *five*.

More rhymes: alive, dive, arrive, strive.

Teddy Bear, Teddy Bear Turn Around

Teddy bear, teddy bear turn around
Teddy bear, teddy bear touch the ground
Teddy bear, teddy bear show your shoe
Teddy bear, teddy bear that will do
Teddy bear, teddy bear go up stairs
Teddy bear, teddy bear say your prayers
Teddy bear, teddy bear turn out the light
Teddy bear, teddy bear say good-night

Listen for the rhyming words: *light* and *night*.

More rhymes: kite, sight, bite, height.

Here Is the Church

Here is the church
Here is the steeple
Open the doors
And see all the people
They stand up to sing
They kneel down to pray
And when the bell rings
They all run away

Listen for the rhyming words: *pray* and *away*.

More rhymes: stay, bay, way, day.

I'm a Little Teapot

I'm a little teapot short and stout
Here is my handle. Here is my spout.
When I get all steamed up, hear me shout
Tip me over and pour me out

Listen for the rhyming words: *shout* and *out*.

More rhymes: pout, doubt, trout, snout.

Way Up in the Apple Tree

Way up in the apple tree
Two little apples were waiting for me
So I shook and I shook and I shook that tree
'Til all those apples came down to me

Listen for the rhyming words: *tree* and *me*.

More rhymes: free, knee, ski, bee.

Chapter 11

Stories and Action Rhymes with Activities and Patterns

As a transition between books or as a rest activity, stories and action rhymes are ideal. They capture the attention of the children and allow them to participate through movement. As the stories become familiar, the children often enjoy helping you tell the story or recite the rhyme.

The patterns included with these stories and rhymes can be used to create magnet or flannel board figures, stick puppets or finger puppets. If the group is small, the children may be invited to help with manipulating these visual aids.

Repeating these stories and rhymes helps the adults in storytime to build vocabulary. With repetition, these stories become very familiar. Once they are familiar, the adults will feel confident to repeat the story or rhyme at home with their child. It is helpful to give a copy of the story and accompanying patterns to each family to take home. Because telling stories and rhymes is so much fun, families often enjoy them as a bedtime or playtime activity. As they repeat these activities at home, they will be reinforcing their command of English.

Five Baby Dragons—Action Rhyme

*Use the pattern to make flannel board or magnet board figures. Begin with all five dragons displayed. As you recite the rhyme, remove one dragon at a time. Ask the children to hold up five fingers. As each dragon flies away they can fold one finger down into the palm of their hand. This action rhyme can be used as a discussion starter for **colors**, **counting**, **playtime**, or **baby animals**. It reinforces narrative skill and phonological awareness.*

Five baby dragons playing at the shore.
The blue one flew away so then there were four.
Four baby dragons climbing a tall tree.
The red one flew away so then there were three.
Three baby dragons cooking up some stew.
The green one flew away so then there were two.
Two baby dragons basking in the sun.
The pink one flew away so then there was one.
One baby dragon playing with his ball.
He flew away, too. No dragons at all.

Mouse Goes Out—Story

*This retelling of an old folk tale can be a discussion starter about **homes** and **neighborhoods**, **staying safe**, and **friendship**. Storytelling reinforces narrative skill. Use the pattern to make flannel board or magnet board figures to illustrate the story.*

Once upon a time a little mouse went out to see the world. He packed some bread and cheese in a basket to eat along the way. He locked the door of his house and walked down the road.

He walked a long, long way. He passed a yellow house, a blue house, and a green house. They were the last three houses on his street. He walked out into the countryside where he had never been before. He walked past tall trees. He walked beside long fences. When he was tired out he stopped to eat his bread and cheese.

After a rest, the mouse walked some more. He came to a little house with a fence. It did not look like the houses on his street. He walked through the gate, and there in the yard he saw two animals he had never seen before.

One of the animals was large, soft, and furry. It had four legs and a long tail. On its face were long white whiskers. The creature was sleeping in the shade of a tree. "How wise and gentle this creature seems," thought the mouse. But he did not wake it up.

The other strange animal had two legs. It had red, yellow and brown feathers sticking out all over. It had a mean face and a sharp yellow beak. It had beady black eyes that stared at the little mouse. "This creature is dangerous!" cried the mouse. He ran as fast as he could. The strange creature chased after him making a horrible noise. "Cock-a-doodle-doo!"

At last the mouse found a hole in the wall. He wiggled and squeezed through the hole and saw three faces staring at him. This time they were mouse faces. "Where did you come from?" asked one of the mice.

"I've come . . . from . . . far . . . away," he gasped. "Where am I now?"

The three mice gathered around him and answered one at a time.

"This is our home."

"We are field mice."

"Tell us what happened."

The little mouse told them about his journey and the two creatures he met in the yard. "One was a harmless creature with pretty fur and whiskers. The other was very mean and was covered in feathers."

The three mice laughed. "You are safe now," said one. "Stay for tea," said another.

"Good thing you got away," said the third mouse. "You were in more danger than you knew. The creature with the feathers is a rooster. He will never hurt a mouse. But the other strange animal with the pretty fur and whiskers is the cat! If he had seen you, you would not be here sharing our tea, that's for sure."

So the little mouse had tea with his three new friends. When he was finished he wiped his paws and said, "Thank you." The little mouse continued on his way more carefully. Now he understood that not every pretty creature is gentle, and not every scary creature is a danger.

Singing Tonight—Action Rhyme

This action rhyme can be used as a discussion starter for **nighttime**, **animal sounds**, **friendship**, *and* **nature walks**. *The rhyme reinforces phonological awareness, and also narrative skill. Use the pattern to make stick figures with Popsicle sticks, or to make magnet of flannel board figures.*

The frogs in the pond are singing tonight.
Croak, croak, croak! Croak, croak, croak.
They sing to their friends in the pale moonlight.
All through the night.

The owls in the trees are singing tonight.
Whoo, whoo whoo. Whoo, whoo, whoo.
They sing to their friends in the pale moonlight.
All through the night.

The crickets in the grass are singing tonight.
Chir, chir, chir. Chir, chir, chir.
They sing to their friends in the pale moonlight.
All through the night.

The Tortoise and the Hare—
Story in Rhyme

A Retelling of an Aesop Fable

*This story can be used to start a discussion about opposites including **fast and slow**. It will also work for a discussion on **friendship** or **honesty**. Use the patterns to make flannel board or magnet board figures.*

Once there was a speedy hare
Who rushed and rushed from here to there.
He claimed that he could not be beat.
Nothing was faster than his feet.

Then a tortoise, slow and steady
Said, "I'll race you. Are you ready?"
All their friends came to the race.
Hare and tortoise took their place.

Like a speedy lightning flash
The hare began his prideful dash.
Then down the road he slowed to a trot.
Then he stopped to rest awhile. Why not?

The hare stretched out and yawned and blinked.
He fell asleep. And while he winked
The tortoise, with his steady pace
Passed him up, and won the race!

Too late the hare woke up and ran.
When he came to the finish line
The tortoise was already there.
"How could a tortoise beat a hare?"

The hare still runs from here to there,
For he is still a speedy hare.
But he doesn't brag about his pace,
For slow and steady won the race.

Two Best Friends—Action Rhyme

Copy the finger puppet patterns and give a set to each person. Children will enjoy moving their hands and placing them behind their back. This rhyme goes well with a discussion on **friendship** *or* **playtime**. *The rhyme reinforces phonological awareness.*

Two best friends went out to play.
> *(Hold up finger puppets on fingers of each hand.)*

One named Jeff and one named Jay.
> *(Wiggle each finger puppet.)*

Run home, Jeff. Run home, Jay.
> *(Put left hand behind back. Put right hand behind back.)*

Come back, Jeff. Come back, Jay.
> *(Bring hands to front again.)*

Piggy Bank—Action Rhyme

This action rhyme allows the children to stand up and use large motor skills to participate, which burns up some energy and helps them get ready to sit for another book. You can use the pattern on the magnet board to introduce the activity. This action rhyme reinforces numbers vocabulary and phonological awareness.

(Stand tall and hold up five fingers.)

> Five shiny nickels
> One by one
> Drop into the piggy bank.
> Oh, what fun.

(Squat down and tap floor with both hands, and then stand. Repeat for numbers one through five.)

> One for a jingle
> Two for a wish
> Three for a jangle
> Four for a fish
> Five for some ice cream in a dish.

Happy Puppy—Action Rhyme

This action rhyme allows the children to move their hands as they sit in place to participate. Movement helps the children burn up some energy and get ready to sit for another book. You can use the pattern on the magnet board to introduce the activity. This action rhyme reinforces vocabulary and phonological awareness.

I have a happy puppy
  (Put hands up like paws.)
He likes to chase a ball
  (Form ball with hands.)
My happy little puppy
  (Put hands up like paws.)
Comes running when I call
  (Pat hands on lap.)

I have a sleepy puppy
  (Yawn.)
He wants to take a nap
  (Rest face on hands.)
My sleepy little puppy
  (Yawn.)
Is curled up in my lap
  (Put arms in lap.)

The Tabby Cat—Action Rhyme

*This action rhyme allows the children to move their hands to participate, which burns up some energy and helps them get ready to sit for another book. As you recite the rhyme pat your hands on your lap to the rhythm of the rhyme. Be sure to draw out and emphasize the word "PIE." You can use the pattern on the magnet board to introduce the activity. This action rhyme can be used to start a discussion about **trains, cats**, or **favorite kinds of pie**. It reinforces vocabulary and phonological awareness.*

A tabby cat
In a coat and hat
Down by the railroad track
He sat

The train came by
The cat waved "hi"
Then he went to the diner
To have some PIE!

The Bear with Honey-Colored Hair— Action Rhyme

This action rhyme allows the children to clap their hands to participate, which burns up some energy and helps them get ready to sit for another book. You can use the pattern on the magnet board to introduce the activity. Children will enjoy taking it home as a color page. Use this rhyme with discussions about **clothes**, **animals**, **dancing** *and* **manners**. *This action rhyme reinforces vocabulary and phonological awareness.*

(Clap on the last three words of each line.)

Once there was a bear, bear, bear
With honey-colored hair, hair, hair.
He wore blue underwear, wear, wear.
The other bears would stare, stare, stare.

One day he went to France, France, France,
And bought a pair of pants, pants, pants.
And now he loves to dance, dance, dance,
Each time he gets a chance, chance, chance.

And now the bears don't stare, stare, stare,
At the funny little bear, bear, bear,
With honey-colored hair, hair, hair,
And bright blue underwear, wear, wear.

The Wind, the Sun, and the Whistling Traveler—Story

A Retelling of an Aesop Fable

*This story can be used with a discussion about **friendship, strength**, or **nature walks**. Teach the rhyming phrases and let the children and adults join in. Use the pattern to make flannel or magnet board figures to illustrate the story. Children will enjoy taking the picture home as a color sheet.*

The Wind and the Sun were old friends. As you know, friends sometimes do not get along. One day they argued about who was stronger.

The Wind said:
"I can blow the trees until they drop their leaves.
I can blow the seas until the waves rise high.
I can blow the rooftop from the castle of a king.
No one, no one is stronger than I!"

The Sun said:
"Until I rise, the day does not begin.
Unless I shine, the seeds do not sprout.
Without my light, no one has sight.
No one is stronger than I, no doubt."

They could not agree! Finally they decided to settle the matter with a challenge. The Wind spotted a traveler walking down a dusty road. "There is the perfect challenge for us," he said. "The first one to make that traveler remove his coat is the strongest."

"As you wish," said the Sun. "You may try first." So the Sun hid behind a cloud and watched as the Wind began to blow.

First a gentle breeze brushed across the traveler's face and tugged at his coat. The traveler buttoned his coat tighter. So the Wind blew harder, one gust stronger than the last. The traveler buttoned all of the buttons and tied the belt of his coat. The stronger the gust, the tighter he held! "I cannot blow his coat off," said the Wind. "See if you can do better."

The Sun took his turn. At first, he only peeked out from behind the cloud. Little by little, he showed his full face. The traveler soon found it too hot to walk with his coat on. He took it off, put it over his shoulder, and went whistling down the road.

Chapter 12

Ready-to-Use Storytime Plans by Theme

This chapter includes 25 storytime plans that are designed for Family Literacy Storytimes. Each of these storytime plans includes an introduction with a visual aid, activity, or conversation starter that will help to put your group at ease. Each theme includes a bibliography of selected picture books with extended learning activities, allowing the storyteller to plan a storytime that meets the needs of the group. The games and activities are designed to help parents and children build confidence in conversational English. A sample storytime plan is included for each theme. Each sample storytime plan focuses on one pre-literacy skill and includes suggested books to share, along with songs, rhymes, stories, and handouts for a complete storytime experience.

A DOG'S LIFE

Introduction

Some dogs are considered pets and part of the family. They are well fed, they sleep inside the house, and may be dressed in sweaters when they go for a walk. Other dogs are working animals. They help to tend sheep or cattle. They eat and sleep outdoors but they are well cared for by their owners. Some dogs wander around free, finding food wherever they can. This storytime introduces the topic of the relationship between dogs and people. You may find that it starts an interesting conversation with your Family Literacy Storytime participants.

Books to Share with Extended Learning Activities

Rankin, Laura. *Fluffy and Baron.* Dial, 2006.

A farm dog called Baron befriends a small yellow duckling called Fluffy. They share food, play together, and chase squirrels through the summer and autumn. Winter passes, and in the spring Fluffy is a grown white duck and watches with interest when three wild ducks land on the pond. How will this affect the friendship between dog and duck?

Literacy Features: Vocabulary, print motivation

Extended Learning Activities:

- Counting activity: Count the eggs in Fluffy's nest. Count the ducklings that are playing with Fluffy and Baron.
- Discuss the talents of Fluffy, Baron, and the children at storytime: Fluffy is good at (hide-and-seek, snapping flies); Baron is good at (tag, squirrel chasing). I am good at . . .
- Ask the parents to tell something that their child is good at.

Hornsey, Chris. *Why Do I Have to Eat off the Floor?* Walker, 2007.

A series of questions usually asked by a child are very funny when asked by a loveable dog, Murphy.

Literacy Features: Vocabulary, print motivation

Extended Learning Activities:

- Reinforce comprehension by asking the children to talk about good manners for dogs and children. Is it good manners for a dog to take a bath? Is it good manners for a child to take a bath? Is it good manners for a dog to eat off the floor? Is it good manners for a child to eat off the floor?
- Strengthen oral fluency by asking the children questions such as: Can a dog learn how to drive a car? What can a dog learn to do? (fetch a ball, protect the baby, bark when someone comes to the house).

Rosen, Michael J. *With a Dog Like That, a Kid Like Me.* Puffin, 2002.

A boy compares his dog to a lion, a croc, a kangaroo, and more.

Literacy Features: Vocabulary, phonological awareness

Extended Learning Activities:

- Reinforce letter knowledge with this activity. On the pony page, point to the letter P. Now ask the children if they can find another word on the page that starts with P (prances). Repeat with seal (slick, soap, sudsy) and beaver (branch).
- Is it bigger or smaller? Revisit each page of the book and ask is a pony bigger or smaller than a dog? Is a seal bigger or smaller than a dog? Ask a parent and child to stand up. Ask the group which is bigger and which is smaller. Now compare two children. Who is bigger?

Wild, Margaret. *The Pocket Dogs.* Scholastic, 2001.

Two small dogs go out every day riding in Mr. Pocket's coat pockets, until the day a small hole in the pocket grows bigger and one little dog falls out. Now all he sees is legs. Lots and lots of legs!

Literacy Features: Narrative skills, print motivation

Extended Learning Activities:

- Print motivation is interest and enjoyment of books. Tell the children what you liked about the story.
- Talk about Biff's bad dream. He dreamed he was lost. Did Biff feel scared?
- Biff had lots of help finding Mr. Pockets. Who carried him in a basket? Who put him in a doll carriage? Who put him in a shopping cart? Where did Biff really want to ride?

Sample Storytime Plan

Theme: A Dog's Life—relationship between dogs and people

Presentation Dates: _____

Literacy Skill Focus: Vocabulary

Books:

> *Fluffy and Baron* by Laura Rankin
> *Why Do I Have to Eat off the Floor?* by Chris Hornsey

Extended Learning Activities:

- Discussion of talents of Fluffy, Baron, and children
- Discussion: What can a dog learn to do?
- Patterned sentences to write on the white board:
    I like to eat cereal. Dogs like to eat dog food.
    I like to play in the park. Dogs like to walk in the park.
    I like to bounce a ball. Dogs like to fetch a ball.
    I like to take a bath. Dogs do not like to take a bath.

Songs, Rhymes, and Rhyming Stories:

Opening: Time for Storytime (p. 47)

Happy Puppy (p. 82)
Raise Them High (p. 44)

Jack Be Nimble (p. 55)

Closing: Goodbye for Now (p. 38)

Handouts:

Happy Puppy coloring page (p. 83)

ALL YEAR LONG

Introduction

The change of seasons is exciting for children. Some members of your Family Literacy Storytime group may come from a part of the world where the seasons are different from where they are living now. Ask questions that can start a conversation about which months of the year are hot, which months are rainy, which months are cold, etc. You may use this storytime theme to teach vocabulary such as months of the year or the names of the seasons.

Books to Share with Extended Learning Activities

Roth, Susan L. *My Love for You All Year Round.* Dial, 2003.

Two mice, parent and child, celebrate their love for the seasons and each other all through the year.

Literacy Features: Vocabulary, print awareness

Extended Learning Activities:

- Print awareness is noticing print and how to follow the written word on a page. Turn the pages again and point to the words JANUARY, FEBRUARY, MARCH, etc., and have the children say them with you.
- Reinforce the vocabulary by asking, "Which month makes you think of hearts? Fireworks? Pumpkins?"

Day, Nancy Raines. *A Kitten's Year.* HarperTrophy, 2001.

A kitten explores the sights, sounds, and smells of the world around it as it grows into a cat.

Literacy Features: Print motivation, vocabulary

Extended Learning Activities:

- The beautiful illustrations of this book are good conversation starters. What is the kitten looking at in the pool? What is the kitten playing with in this picture?
- Have the children act out the verbs in a kitten-like way: peeks, toys, stalks, paws, tumbles, etc.

Tudor, Tasha. *Around the Year.* Simon & Schuster, 2001 (reprint).

This rhymed story depicts a year of activities set in rural America of a quieter and simpler time.

Literacy Features: Rhyme, phonological awareness, vocabulary

Extended Learning Activities:

- Read a rhymed couplet and emphasize the rhyme and then see if the children can add another rhyming word or two. For example: joys, boys toys; or fair, air, hair, stair, chair.
- Explain and talk about some of the unfamiliar vocabulary such as apple roasting, new-mown hay, and swallows southward fly. Ask one or two of the parents to tell about something they enjoyed doing when they were small.

Appelt, Kathi. *A Red Wagon Year.* Harcourt, 1996.

A red wagon is a favorite toy, and it has a new purpose for every month of the year.

Literacy Features: Vocabulary, print motivation

Extended Learning Activities:

- Show your enjoyment of this book by talking about activities you enjoy that are illustrated in it, such as feeding the birds, going to the beach and growing vegetables in a garden.
- Explore vocabulary by asking, "How can the red wagon be a table? How can it be a bathtub or a tractor?"

Sample Storytime Plan

Theme: All Year Long—the change of seasons

Presentation Dates: _____

Literacy Skill Focus: Print awareness

Books:

> *My Love for You All Year Round* by Susan L. Roth
> *Around the Year* by Tasha Tudor

Extended Learning Activities:

- Point to the words on the page and say the names of the months.
- Hold the book upside down. Point to the cover and ask, "Is this the right way to hold the book?"
- Show that reading English goes from left to right by moving your finger left to right as you read the title of the book.
- Tell the group the month you were born in. Write it on the white board. Ask which month it is right now. Write it on the white board.

Songs, Rhymes, and Rhyming Stories:

Opening: Time for Storytime (p. 47)

Humpty Dumpty (p. 59)
I'm a Little Teapot (p. 66)
The Wind, the Sun, and the Whistling Traveler (p. 88)

Closing: Goodbye for Now (p. 38)

Handouts:

The Wind, the Sun, and the Whistling Traveler story and pictures (pp. 88–89)

AMAZING MOTHERS

Introduction

This storytime includes books about many different kinds of mothers. The mothers in your storytime group may enjoy talking about their hobbies or work, or showing a treasured possession to the storytime group.

Books to Share with Extended Learning Activities

Browne, Anthony. *My Mom.* Farrar Straus Giroux, 2005.

From baking cakes with monkey faces, to singing like an angel or roaring like a lion, this mom can do almost anything. She could be a dancer, an astronaut, or a film star. This supermom is really nice, and full of love.

Literacy Features: Vocabulary, print motivation

Extended Learning Activities:

- Astronaut Mom counting activity: Practice counting backward from 10 to 1 with the children. Blow up a balloon but don't tie a knot. Have a helper hold the end while you draw a face on it with a black marker. Tell the children that this astronaut mom will blast off when you count down from 10. Lead the countdown very dramatically! When you arrive at one, release the balloon. It will fly around the room, causing lots of laughter.
- For oral fluency, talk about the kinds of things that a real SUPERMOM could do. Could she jump as high as the moon? Could she carry 100 pizzas on her head? Could she run faster than a train? Try for silly ideas, the sillier the better. Now ask one or two of the mothers to tell of a super skill that they wish they had.

Ashman, Linda. *Mama's Day.* Simon & Schuster, 2006.

Mamas everywhere play games with babies, give them snacks, sing songs, keep them safe, and do what mamas do: loving babies every minute.

Literacy Features: Vocabulary, phonological awareness

Extended Learning Activities:

- Creative dramatics: Lead the children through a morning of taking care of baby as they pantomime picking up the baby, giving the baby a bath, pushing baby in a swing, etc.
- Ask each mother to name a part of her daily routine. For example: "I shop for food. I wash the dishes. I make lunch for my child."

Lasky, Kathryn. *Mommy's Hands.* Hyperion, 2002.

A mother's hands can pour milk without spilling, untangle shoelace knots, braid hair, knead dough, teach printing, and point out the constellations, among other amazing abilities.

Literacy Features: Print motivation, vocabulary

Extended Learning Activities:

- Count the freckles: Draw a face with lots of freckles on the white board. Let the children count them with you.
- Sing the traditional song "Here We Go 'Round the Mulberry Bush." Include verses in the song such as this is the way we knead the dough, pour the milk, braid the hair, etc.

Winter, Jeanette. *Angelina's Island.* Farrar, Straus, and Giroux, 2007.

Every day, Angelina dreams of her home in Jamaica and imagines she is there, until her mother finds a wonderful way to convince her that New York is now their home.

Literacy Features: Print awareness, narrative skill

Extended Learning Activities:

- Ask the families to share something they like about home, either their home here or the home they left. They may describe the food, the climate, the music, or other cultural features that they enjoy.
- Ask the children to tell you what Angelina's mother did that made her happy. Then ask: "What does your mother do to make you happy?"

Sample Storytime Plan

Theme: Amazing Mothers—the wonderful things mothers can do

Presentation Dates: _____

Literacy Skill Focus: Vocabulary

Books:

Mommy's Hands by Kathryn Lasky
Mama's Day by Linda Ashman

Extended Learning Activities:

- Ask each mother to name a part of her daily routine. For example: "I shop for food. I wash the dishes. I make lunch for my child."
- Patterned sentences to write on the white board:

My mother has long hair.	My mother has white teeth.
My mother has soft hands.	My mother has strong arms.
My mother has green eyes.	

Songs, Rhymes, and Rhyming Stories:

Opening: Time for Storytime (p. 47)

I'm a Little Teapot (p. 66)
Family (p. 37)
There Was an Old Woman Who Lived in a Shoe (p. 57)

Closing: Goodbye for Now (p. 38)

Handouts:

Family song (p. 37)

ANIMAL MAMA AND CHILD

Introduction

Reading about the warmth and love between animal families can start a conversation about how human mothers care for their children. Be sure to mention how wonderful the mothers in your Family Literacy Storytime group are because they bring their child to the library and read to their child.

Books to Share with Extended Learning Activities

Jennings, Sharon. *Bearcub and Mama.* Kids Can, 2005.

As Bearcub grows, he learns many things from Mama Bear. When a winter storm spills out of the sky, Bearcub is lost! Can he remember what Mama taught him to do?

Literacy Features: Narrative skill, print awareness

Extended Learning Activities:

- Narrative skill: Retell the story using a large teddy bear and a smaller teddy bear. Have the children pantomime the actions. Bearcub follows Mama down to the river to catch a fish, across the meadow, and up a tree to find honey. Then he plays in the cornfield, and slides on the ice and gets lost. Bearcub howls for Mama. He covers his eyes with his paws, he crawls into his den to wait for Mama. In the morning she is there.
- Print awareness: Show the cover of the book. Ask the children to point to the picture of Bearcub. Then point to the word on the cover. Repeat for the picture and word for Mama.

McBratney, Sam. *I Love It When You Smile.* HarperCollins, 2005.

A small kangaroo wasn't in the smiling mood, not even when his mother tickled him and played with him. But when his mom slipped into a muddy hole, Roo just had to smile.

Literacy Features: Print motivation, phonological awareness

Extended Learning Activities:

- Play with the fun language from this book by acting out: Slippity, slippity, slide, slop.
- Rhymes with Roo: Play with the name for the main character of the book. Think of rhymes for Roo. For example: shoe, blue, stew, few, boo, do, glue, new.
- Ask the parents to make a funny face that will make their child smile or laugh.

Stutson, Caroline. *Mama Loves You.* Cartwheel, 2005.

I am yours; you are mine; Mama loves you, Porcupine! From a porcupine to a butterfly, a polar bear to a mouse, each young animal has the unconditional love of its mother.

Literacy Features: Phonological awareness, print awareness

Extended Learning Activities:

- Predicting: Read the book a second time and let the parents and children complete the rhymes from the picture clues.

- Print awareness activity: Show that reading goes left to right by pointing to the words as you read a few of the pages.

Mallat, Kathy. *Mama Love.* Walker, 2004.

A young chimp describes his mama as "quite inventive, strong, and brave, and very attentive." In return, the chimp loves his mama: "She is the twinkle in my eye, my heart's pitter-patter, my star in the sky."

Literacy Features: Print motivation, vocabulary

Extended Learning Activities:

- Strengthen print awareness by pointing out individual words on the page. The big bold type of this book is easy to see.
- Creative dramatics: Let the children play like a chimp as you ask questions. For example, "Can you jump like a chimp? Can you reach up high like a chimp?"

Sample Storytime Plan

Theme: Animal Mama and Child—the warmth and love between animal families

Presentation Dates: _____

Literacy Skill Focus: Narrative skill

Books:

Bearcub and Mama by Sharon Jennings
I Love It When You Smile by Sam McBratney

Extended Learning Activities:

- Retell *Bearcub and Mama* using teddy bears. Ask "What happened next?"
- Lead a pantomime of mama kangaroo and baby kangaroo going through their day. Ask "Did baby kangaroo smile?" Baby kangaroo does not smile until mama slips in the mud. Smile broadly and praise the children for their big smiles.
- Model oral fluency and narrative skill by talking about your day so far, such as, "This morning I had to look for my shoes. I found them under my bed. I had toast for breakfast. I fed my cat. Then I came to storytime."

Songs, Rhymes, and Rhyming Stories:

Opening: Time for Storytime (p. 47)

Two Little Black Birds (p. 62)
Someday I Would (p. 45)
Two Best Friends (p. 78)

Closing: Goodbye for Now (p. 38)

Handouts:

Two Best Friends pattern and story (pp. 78–79)

BAKING TOGETHER

Introduction

Baking treats and pastries is a bonding experience for families. It is also educational, because it involves conversation and measuring. You may wish to bring treats that are mentioned in the books you read for this storytime. Encourage your group to talk about treats they like to make together. Give recipes for parents and children to make together at home. This encourages measuring, reading, and vocabulary practice.

Books to Share with Extended Learning Activities

Andreasen, Dan. *Baker's Dozen.* Henry Holt, 2007.

The baker bakes one cream éclair, two German chocolate cakes, and many more treats. Then 13 people flock to the bakery to buy them.

Literacy Features: Vocabulary, letter knowledge, phonological awareness

Extended Learning Activities:

- The pastries in this book may be unfamiliar to your group. You may want to bring in samples from the bakery so everyone can try them. Encourage the group to talk about treats they enjoy.
- Practice letter recognition of letters B and D for Bakers and Dozen by indicating them on the cover of the book. Ask for anyone whose name begins with B or D. Write the names on the white board.
- Phonological awareness game: I see something that starts with B. Look around the room, select an object that starts with letter B. Ask for guesses until someone gets it right. Repeat a few times.

Kleven, Elisa. *Sun Bread.* Dutton, 2001.

On a gray snowy day, a baker makes a treat that cheers everyone up.

Literacy Features: Vocabulary

Extended Learning Activities:

- Name the animal friends: Show the double-page spread in the center of the book and see how many of the animals the children can name.
- Creative play: Use play dough to form suns, stars, and animal shapes.
- Give parents a recipe for play dough that they can make at home.

Pinkney, Jerry. *The Little Red Hen.* Dial, 2006.

Little Red Hen asks her animal neighbors to help her feed her family. From planting the wheat seeds, to baking the bread, everyone answers, "Not I." When the bread is ready, who gets to eat it?

Literacy Features: Narrative skill, vocabulary

Extended Learning Activities:

- Encourage the children to join in when you read the phrase "Not I."
- Narrative skill activity: Help the children retell the story through questioning.

What happens when you plant a wheat seed?

What do you do with the wheat after it grows?

How does the wheat get made into flour?

What did the Little Red Hen make out of the flour?

- Color vocabulary activity: The text is printed in colors that match the animals. Identify the colors and match them with the illustrations of the animals.
- Animal vocabulary activity: Point to one of the animal neighbors and tell what it is. Ask children to make the sound of each animal.
- Numbers vocabulary: How many chicks does Little Red Hen have? Count them together.

Smalls, Irene. *My Pop Pop and Me.* Little, Brown, 2006.

A young boy bakes a lemon cake with his grandfather. First he puts on a chef's hat, then he washes his hands, and then the baking begins! Recipe for Lemon Bar Cake included on last page of the book.

Literacy Features: Phonological awareness, vocabulary

Extended Learning Activities:

- Phonological awareness rhyme activity: Ask for rhymes for several words in the book, such as Pop Pop, sniff, peel, dip, pour.
- Kitchen vocabulary: Point to the baking tools and say the words.
- Oral fluency: Ask for discussion of foods that they like to make together at home.

Sample Storytime Plan

Theme: Baking Together—a bonding experience for families

Presentation Dates: _____

Literacy Skill Focus: Vocabulary

Books:

The Little Red Hen by Jerry Pinkney
My Pop Pop and Me by Irene Smalls

Extended Learning Activities:

- Color vocabulary: text and animals in *The Little Red Hen*
- Kitchen tools vocabulary: bring bowls, spoons, pans, measuring cups to show

Songs, Rhymes, and Rhyming Stories:

Opening: Time for Storytime (p. 47)

Song: See What I Can Do (tune: This Old Man)

> You see me, I see you
> Watch and see what I can do
> I can clap my hands and
> I can touch my shoe
> Lots of things that I can do.

You see me, I see you
Watch and see what I can do
I can wiggle my fingers and
I can wave to you
Lots of things that I can do.

Little Jack Horner (p. 61)
My Meals (p. 42)
I'm a Little Teapot (p. 66)

Closing: Goodbye for Now (p. 38)

Handouts:

Scented Colored Play Dough Recipe or Oatmeal Raisin Cookies Recipe (see Appendix)

BIG, BIG ANIMALS

Introduction

Introduce this storytime by talking about big and small. Show your shoe and compare it to a child's shoe. Show a parent's hand and compare it to a child's hand. Show a small tennis ball next to a large beach ball. Now ask the children to imagine a small animal. What are they thinking of? A rabbit, a mouse, a kitten, or a bird perhaps. Then ask them to imagine a big, big animal. What are they thinking of? A bear, a horse, a whale, or an elephant.

Books to Share with Extended Learning Activities

Newman, Jeff. *Hippo! No, Rhino.* Little, Brown, 2006.

A careless worker at the zoo places the wrong sign near the rhino's cage, causing zoo visitors to mistake it for a hippo.

Literacy Features: Print motivation

Extended Learning Activities:

- Reading signs: Show pictures of a stop sign, an exit sign, and an open sign. Many of the children will recognize them and be able to read them. Now show the pictures in the book of the hippo sign and the rhino sign. Can the children read them?
- Print motivation is enjoyment and excitement about reading. Bring several print formats other than books to show, such as a newspaper, a magazine, a map, or a phone book. Talk about how you use and enjoy these tools.
- Follow the signs game: Make a few signs that read walk, stop, trash, and sit. After showing the signs and teaching their meaning, lead the group on an imaginary walk around the neighborhood, to the corner store, the playground, or to the zoo. When you are crossing the street, be sure to stop at the corner where you see the stop sign. And wait until you see the walk sign before crossing. Buy a candy bar and throw the wrapper into the trash. Once you are at the park or the zoo, find a park bench and sit for awhile.

Bachelet, Gilles. *My Cat, the Silliest Cat in the World.* Abrams, 2006.

This cat likes to take naps on the couch, eat his food from a bowl, and keep clean just like most other cats. But this cat also has a trunk!

Literacy Features: Print motivation, narrative skill

Extended Learning Activities:

- Ask the children if the animal in this book is really a cat. How do they know it is not a cat? What kind of animal is it? How do they know?
- Silly cat! Turn the pages a second time and explain what the "cat" is doing. For example, "Here is the cat sleeping on the television." Encourage the kids to say "Silly cat" for each page. The more giggles the better.

Wilson, Karma. *Hilda Must Be Dancing*. McElderry, 2004.

Hilda Hippo loves to dance, but the other animals beg her to find a quieter hobby.

Literacy Features: Print motivation, narrative skill, phonological awareness

Extended Learning Activities:

- Encourage the children to dance as you repeat some of the rhythm phrases from this book. Swisha-swisha Clap! Clap! Jump, jump, jump!
- Ask the parents and children to talk about their hobbies and activities. Do they enjoy singing, swimming, or drawing? How about dancing?

Anderson, Derek. *Gladys Goes Out to Lunch*. Simon & Schuster, 2005.

At the zoo, Gladys always eats bananas. One day Gladys smells something even better than bananas. So Gladys follows her nose outside of the zoo, looking for the smell at a pizzeria, a French café, and even an ice cream stand. Can you guess what the delicious food is that Gladys wants?

Literacy Features: Letter knowledge, narrative skill

Extended Learning Activities:

- Gladys tries pizzas with pepperoni, pesto, and pineapple. What is the beginning sound of each of these words? Can you think of any more foods that begin with the sound "P"? (peanuts, popcorn, pretzels, pudding).
- Gladys tries fancy French food including frog's legs, fried snails, and frozen mousse. Can you think of more foods that begin with the sound "F"? (french fries, frosting, Fritos).

Sample Storytime Plan

Theme: Big, Big Animals—giants from all over the world

Presentation Dates: _____

Literacy Skill Focus: Print motivation

Books:

My Cat, the Silliest Cat in the World by Gilles Bachelet
Hilda Must Be Dancing by Karma Wilson

Extended Learning Activities:

- Show a map, a newspaper, or a magazine and talk about how reading these helps you.
- Show the cover of the book before reading. Point to the title. Point to the author's name. Ask "Do you know what an author does? He/she writes books."
- After reading a book say, "I loved this book because . . ." (finish the sentence). Invite a few parents or children to finish the sentence, too.
- Patterned sentences to write on the white board:

   I have a big brother.
   I have a big smile.
   I have a big family.
   I have a big dog.

I have a small nose.
I have a small toe.
I have a small box.
I have a small cat.

Songs, Rhymes, and Rhyming Stories:

Opening: Time for Storytime (p. 47)

Teddy Bear Teddy Bear Turn Around (p. 64)
Would You Like to Fly? (p. 50)
I'm a Little Teapot (p. 66)
Hey Diddle Diddle (p. 54)

Closing: Goodbye for Now (p. 38)

Handouts:

Hey Diddle Diddle coloring page (p. 54)

BOYS AND GIRLS

Introduction

Boys and girls like to play! All over the world, children invent games and find interesting ways to explore their world. Your Family Literacy Storytime group might like to talk about some of their favorite toys or games. Try to get the parents to talk about what they enjoyed doing as children. It may be surprising how similar the favorite games are between boys and girls, adults and children.

Books to Share with Extended Learning Activities

Browne, Anthony. *Silly Billy*. Candlewick, 2006.

Billy worries about everything, but Grandma has just the thing for a boy like Billy.

Literacy Features: Vocabulary, print awareness

Extended Learning Activities:

- Print awareness activity: On the second reading, show the picture of Billy and the hats. Read the text and point to the large word "HATS" but do not say it. See if the children can supply the word from context. You may also try this with "SHOES" and "CLOUDS", etc.
- Practice family vocabulary: Write Grandma and Grandson on the white board. Ask the group to tell you about other family members such as Mother, Father, Sister, Brother. Write all of their suggested vocabulary words on the white board.
- Count the worry dolls in Grandma's hand. Ask, "If Billy tells one worry to each doll, how many worries will he give away?" (six).

Lewison, Wendy Cheyette. *Two Is for Twins*. Viking, 2006.

Toddler twins celebrate the fun they have together such as wearing matching clothes, riding the seesaw, and having two cakes at their birthday party.

Literacy Features: Phonological awareness, vocabulary

Extended Learning Activities:

- On the second reading, emphasize the rhyme and pause to allow the children to complete the phrase. "Two hands make two to hold a cup. Two eyes look down, two eyes look . . . up."
- Show the cover of the book. Point to the word "Two." Count two children, two bees, two birds, and two snails. Ask "How many dogs are in the wagon?" (one).

Schwartz, Amy. *A Beautiful Girl*. Roaring Book Press, 2006.

On her way to the market, Jenna meets four new friends. They wonder why Jenna does not have a trunk, a beak, lots of eyes, or gills like they have.

Literacy Features: Narrative skill, vocabulary

Extended Learning Activities:

- Oral fluency discussion: Show the picture of the elephant. Ask comparative questions such as, "How many feet does an elephant have? How many do you have? An elephant has big ears. Are your ears big or small?" You may also make comparisons with the robin, fly and goldfish if you wish.

- Vocabulary activity: Parts of the animals' bodies, parts of a human body. Write trunk, beak, gills, etc., on the white board. Write head, arms, hands and face, etc., on the white board.
- Beautiful girl—beautiful name: Show the book and say, "This beautiful girl is Jenna." Then introduce each girl in the room the same way, or ask their parents to introduce them.

Bechdolt, Jack and Yaccarino, Dan. *Little Boy with a Big Horn*. Golden, 2008.

Ollie wants to practice his big horn, but his family doesn't like the noise. So Ollie goes out in a rowboat to practice offshore. When the fog rolls in, Ollie's horn saves a ship from running aground and Ollie is a hero.

Literacy Features: Narrative skill, print motivation

Extended Learning Activities:

- Lead the group in retelling the story by asking leading questions. What does Ollie like to do? Is it loud? Does his family like it? What does Ollie do next? Where does he go to practice?
- Print motivation is the enjoyment of books. Show your enjoyment of this book by using inflection in your voice, pausing for dramatic effect, and lots of facial expressions. Ask questions of the children and talk about what they liked about this book.

Sample Storytime Plan

Theme: Boys and Girls—fun and interesting ways to explore the world

Presentation Dates: _____

Literacy Skill Focus: Narrative skill

Books:

> *Little Boy with a Big Horn* by Bechdolt and Yaccarino
> *A Beautiful Girl* by Amy Schwartz

Extended Learning Activities:

- Form a little band by asking each person to pretend to play a horn, a drum, or the cymbals. Put on some marching music and parade around the room.
- Use toy animals and a doll as characters. Help your group retell *A Beautiful Girl* by asking questions such as "Where was Jenna going?" "Which animal did she meet first?"
- Write human body parts and corresponding animal parts on the white board. For example:

Nose	Trunk
Hair	Feathers
Hands	Fins

Songs, Rhymes, and Rhyming Stories:

> *Opening:* Time for Storytime (p. 47)

Five Baby Dragons (p. 70)
Two Little Black Birds (p. 62)
Someday I Would (p. 45)

Closing: Goodbye for Now (p. 38)

Handouts:

Two Little Black Birds finger puppets (p. 62)

BUSY DAY

Introduction

Ask a series of questions about the sequence of daily activities. This activity builds oral fluency as well as vocabulary and comprehension. What do you do first, set the table or eat lunch? Get into your bed or put on your pajamas? Go to work or eat lunch? Feed the dog or walk the dog? Play with your toys or put away your toys?

Books to Share with Extended Learning Activities

Arquette, Kerry. *What Did You Do Today?* Harcourt, 2002.

On the busy day at the farm bees are buzzing, chicks are pecking, and birds are learning to fly.

Literacy Features: Vocabulary, phonological awareness, letter knowledge

Extended Learning Activities:

- Name the animals: Turn the pages of the book again and ask children to name the animals on the page.
- Ask the children to listen for words that start with the "B" sound such as bees, buzzing, and birds. Do any of their names begin with the "B" sound? Write these words on the white board.
- Oral fluency: Ask questions about the morning activities that took place today before storytime. Try to make them silly. "Did you paint your face with pudding this morning? No, you washed your face." Ask the adults to describe their morning activities.

Millen, C.M. *Blue Bowl Down: An Appalachian Rhyme.* Candlewick, 2004.

Mother and child fetch water from the well, pour it into the blue bowl, add flour, and pat it into dough to make bread. It rests and rises overnight, and in the morning the bread is baked into delicious loaves.

Literacy Features: Vocabulary, phonological awareness, letter knowledge

Extended Learning Activities:

- Point out alliteration through the book: blue bowl, walk the water, light the lantern, etc.
- On the first page, look for words that begin with the letter B: blue, bowl, baby, bread. Write the words on the white board, or show flash cards.
- Turn the pages again and ask the children to act out the verbs: lift, reach, walk, shake, stir, pat, etc. Make sentences with each verb to reinforce comprehension.

Ballard, Robin. *My Day, Your Day.* Greenwillow, 2001.

Inventive parallels are drawn between the activities of child and parent during their busy day. A great conversation starter for families.

Literacy Features: Vocabulary, print awareness

Extended Learning Activities:

- Conversation practice: What is your mommy's job? What is your daddy's job? What is your job? Lead the conversation with children and parents by starting with sentence patterns (I work at home. I work in an office. I work at a store.).

Ormerod, Jan. *Miss Mouse's Day*. HarperCollins, 2001.

An energetic little girl spends the day with her best friend, a mouse doll. The mouse is smeared with paint, dragged through the mud, and even left behind. But by the end of the day the mouse has been found, cleaned up, and well loved.

Literacy Features: Vocabulary, narrative skills

Extended Learning Activities:

- Pantomime the activities of Miss Mouse's day. Read a story. Get dressed. Eat breakfast. Draw a picture, etc.
- Show the pictures of Miss Mouse getting dressed. Ask questions such as, "Why is Miss Mouse too hot wearing this? What would be better? What does "too frilly" mean? Would you like to wear these frilly clothes?"

Sample Storytime Plan

Theme: Busy Day—sequence of daily activities

Presentation Dates: _____

Literacy Skill Focus: Letter knowledge

Books:

> *What Did You Do Today?* by Kerry Arquette
> *Blue Bowl Down: An Appalachian Rhyme* by C.M. Millen

Extended Learning Activities:

- Focus on listening for the "B" sound as in "busy."
- What Did You Do Today? Look for words that start with the "B" sound such as bees, buzzing, and birds.
- Blue Bowl Down: Look for words that begin with the letter B: blue, bowl, baby, bread.
- Favorite things game: Ask your group to name some of their favorite things that begin with the "B" sound. Start with birthday, bubbles, bell, books, bike, bread, bath.
- Letter knowledge activity: Show the letter B on the cover of *Blue Bowl Down*.
- Teach this rhyme:
    B
    B is for butterfly
    B is for breeze
    B is for bird
    Up in the trees.

- Patterned sentences to write on the white board:
  Bees are busy buzzing.
  Bears are busy climbing trees.
  Baby is busy crawling.
  Brother is busy studying.
  Dad is busy mowing the lawn.
  Mom is busy brushing sister's hair.
  I am busy picking up my toys.

Songs, Rhymes, and Rhyming Stories:

Opening: Time for Storytime (p. 47)

Letters (p. 40)
Little Bo-Peep (p. 58)
Two Best Friends (p. 78)
Five Baby Dragons (p. 70)

Closing: Goodbye for Now (p. 38)

Handouts:

Little Bo-Peep coloring page (p. 58) or Two Best Friends finger puppets (p. 79)

COWS

Introduction

If your storytime participants have lived mostly in an urban setting, they may not have seen cows up close. They may recognize the sound a cow makes and they may know that they live on ranches and farms. Guide their imagination by narrating a drive in the country. Pack a picnic lunch, get into the car and fasten your seat belt, and then drive past the stores and the houses until you see lots of green trees and big open fields with some fences. Soon you see a red barn with some animals standing near it. They are big animals, with four legs. You can hear them making a sound. Moooo! Does anybody know what kind of animals they are?

Books to Share with Extended Learning Activities

Willis, Jeanne. *Misery Moo.* Henry Holt, 2003.

A lamb tries to cheer up her friend, a moody old cow.

Literacy Features: Letter knowledge, narrative skill, print awareness

Extended Learning Activities:

- Point to the cover of the book. Show the title, *Misery Moo,* which is written on a dark rain cloud. Ask if the cow on the cover looks happy or sad. Explain that misery is another word for sadness. Show that both misery and moo begin with the letter M.
- Ask questions to encourage retelling of the story. How did the lamb cheer up Misery Moo when it was raining? When it was her birthday? When she was tired of the view?

Roland, Timothy. *Come Down Now, Flying Cow.* Random, 1997.

Beth the cow jumps into a hot air balloon and flies away, starting a hilarious series of mishaps.

Literacy Features: Phonological awareness, narrative skill

Extended Learning Activities:

- Things that fly: Make a list of things that fly, including some found in the book as well as suggestions from the children. Write the list on the white board.
- What would happen if: See if the children can think of some more funny consequences of a cow flying around in a hot air balloon. For example, what would happen if the balloon flew over a school? (It might hit the flagpole.) What would happen if the balloon flew over the North Pole? (It might run into Santa's sleigh.)

Harrison, David. *When Cows Come Home.* Tandem, 2001.

A herd of cows takes off on a holiday and plays tag, rides bicycles, square-dances, and goes swimming when the farmer looks away.

Literacy Features: Print motivation, phonological awareness, letter knowledge

Extended Learning Activities:

- Show the book cover and point to the title. Cows starts with "C." Come starts with "C."
- Act like a cow. Ask the children to stand up and act like a cow as you give them cow-like behaviors such as gently sway, chew your cud, swish your tail, eat some grass, moo.

French, Jackie. *Too Many Pears*. Star Bright Books, 2003.

Pamela will do almost anything to get her favorite food, pears. Amy and her family and friends are afraid no one else will get to eat any. What can they do?

Literacy Features: Letter knowledge, narrative skill

Extended Learning Activities:

- Pamela and pears both start with the "P" sound. Find the letter P on several pages. Ask the group to try to think of more words that start with the letter "P."
- What does Pamela like to eat? How does she get some? What do you like to eat? How do you get some?

Sample Storytime Plan

Theme: Cows—animals that live on ranches and farms

Presentation Dates: _____

Literacy Skill Focus: Letter knowledge

Books:

Misery Moo by Jeanne Willis
Too Many Pears by Jackie French

Extended Learning Activities:

- Misery and moo begin with M. Practice saying moo. What does a cow give us that we like to drink? Milk.
- Pamela and pears begin with P. Can you think of more foods that begin with the letter P?
- Name some farm animals and write them on the white board.

Songs, Rhymes, and Rhyming Stories:

Opening: Time for Storytime (p. 47)

Mary Mary Quite Contrary (p. 56)
Pizza Popcorn Peanuts (p. 43)
My Meals (p. 42)

Closing: Goodbye for Now (p. 38)

Handouts:

Pizza Popcorn Peanuts music (p. 43) or Recipe for Peachy Peanut Pita Sandwich (see Appendix)

ERIC CARLE'S WORLD

Introduction

Eric Carle was born in the United States, but he moved to Germany when he was six years old and he grew up there. Later he moved back to New York to work as an artist. Ask the storytime group to tell where they were born and when they moved to the United States. Eric Carle was first an illustrator, working with Bill Martin Jr. Later he was both the author and the illustrator of many successful picture books. Tell the children that the author thinks of the story and the illustrator creates the pictures. Many of Eric Carle's books are about nature and the world around us. His pictures are bright and colorful, and are created with paper collage.

Books to Share with Extended Learning Activities

Carle, Eric. *Does a Kangaroo Have a Mother, Too?* HarperCollins, 2000.

Animals have a mother, too. Just like me and you.

Literacy Features: Vocabulary

Extended Learning Activities:

- Write the names of some of the animals in this book on the white board. Say the names of the letters as you write them. Point to the corresponding words in the book (written in bold-colored letters).
- Turn the pages of the book a second time and let the children say the names of the animals.

Carle, Eric. *Hello, Red Fox.* Simon and Schuster, 1998.

Little Frog invites several friends to his birthday party, including Red Fox, Purple Butterfly, and Orange Cat. As they begin to arrive, Mama has to look at each one for a long time to see its true color.

Literacy Features: Vocabulary, print awareness

Extended Learning Activities:

- On the last double-page spread of the book, guide the group in naming all of Little Frog's guests.
- *Hello, Red Fox* is printed in red. Read the title, point to the title, and ask what color the letters are. The fox on the cover is not red. Ask what color the fox is. Explain the color theory that the primary colors (red, yellow, and blue) each have a complementary color (green, purple, and orange).

Carle, Eric. *The Very Clumsy Click Beetle.* Philomel, 1999.

A small click beetle tries to learn how to click and flip but he keeps landing on his back. Each animal he meets encourages him to keep trying until at last the click beetle can turn graceful somersaults and land on his feet.

Literacy Features: Vocabulary, print awareness

Extended Learning Activities:

- Pantomime the little click beetle crawling up, down, through, and among.
- Name the animals that the little click beetle meets, including earthworm, turtle, snail, etc.
- Print awareness is recognizing that the story comes from the words in the book. Show that you are reading the words by moving your finger under a few of the lines as you read them.

Martin Jr., Bill. *Baby Bear, Baby Bear, What Do You See?* Henry Holt, 2007.

As Baby Bear searches for Mama, he sees some North American animals such as a mountain goat, a blue heron, and a rattlesnake.

Literacy Features: Vocabulary, phonological awareness

Extended Learning Activities:

- Turn the pages a second time and see if your group can name each new animal.
- Listen for rhyming pairs. Listen for word pairs that begin with the same sound.

Carle, Eric. *Eric Carle's Opposites.* Grosset & Dunlap, 2007.

A beautiful board book with colorful Eric Carle illustrations. Unfold the full-page flaps to explore opposites. Short and tall, big and little, over and under!

Literacy Features: Vocabulary, print motivation

Extended Learning Activities:

- Exploring big and little: Bring two teddy bears, two shoes, two spoons, etc. Hold up the pair and ask the children to tell which is big and which is little.
- Exploring over and under: With a parent for your partner, hold hands and make a bridge that all of the children (and parents?) can walk under. You may want to sing "London bridge is falling down" while you do this activity. Next, set a candle on the floor and let the children jump over it. You may want to recite the rhyme "Jack be nimble, Jack be quick" while you do this activity.

Sample Storytime Plan

Theme: Eric Carle's World—colorful paper collage

Presentation Dates: _____

Literacy Skill Focus: Vocabulary

Books:

Eric Carle's Opposites by Eric Carle
The Very Clumsy Click Beetle by Eric Carle

Extended Learning Activities:

- Explain the meaning of opposite and give several examples. Point to something black and then to something white. Show two spoons, one big and one little. Hold a book over your head, and then hold it under your chair. Ask a parent and child to stand up and point to the tall one and the short one.
- Name the animals that the little click beetle meets, including earthworm, turtle, snail, etc.
- Write them on the white board.

Songs, Rhymes, and Rhyming Stories:

Opening: Time for Storytime (p. 47)

I'm a Little Teapot (p. 66)
Raise Them High (p. 44)
Jack Be Nimble (p. 55)

Closing: Goodbye for Now (p. 38)

Handouts:

Give children some cut tissue paper and a piece of white construction paper so they can make a paper collage at home.

FRIENDS

Introduction

Ask: What is a friend? Some answers may be: A friend is someone to play with. A friend is someone who likes you even when you are acting silly. A friend comes to your birthday party. A friend tries to cheer you up when you are sad. A friend invites you over for lunch. A friend helps you when you have a big job to do.

Books to Share with Extended Learning Activities

Stoeke, Janet. *A Friend for Minerva Louise.* Puffin, 2001.

A loveable hen notices something different about the house with red curtains. She looks for the clues and decides there is a new bunny in the house. Is she right?

Literacy Features: Vocabulary, print motivation

Extended Learning Activities:

- Minerva is confused about the new things in the house. Ask the children to tell you the real name and purpose for each. For example the "wheelbarrow" is really a baby carriage and the "rabbit hutch" is really the baby's crib.
- Play a game called "Where is the baby?" Sit everyone in a circle. Give one person a baby doll. Give another person a toy or paper chicken. Start passing the doll around the circle in one direction. Start passing the chicken around the circle in the other direction. When one person gets both of them everyone cheers because Minerva has found the baby at last.

Heide, Florence Parry. *That's What Friends Are For.* Candlewick, 2007.

Theodore the elephant has hurt his leg and can't meet his cousin at the end of the forest. His friends give plenty of advice because that's what friends are for. Finally, the opossum says, "Friends are to help." And he thinks of a perfect solution.

Literacy Features: Narrative skill, vocabulary

Extended Learning Activities:

- Turn the pages of the book a second time and let the children name the animal friends to reinforce the vocabulary.
- Who is your cousin? Explain to the children that cousins are the children of their parent's brothers or sisters. Ask them if they have cousins.

Simmons, Jane. *Together.* Knopf, 2007.

Two dogs, Mousse and Nut, are best friends. They enjoy walking and playing together. But one day they discover that there are some things they just can't do together. "You're not my best friend anymore," said Mousse unhappily. Will they be able to save their friendship?

Literacy Features: Narrative skill, vocabulary

Extended Learning Activities:

- Sing a slightly different version of an old song:
  Rain, rain go away
  Mousse and Nut want to play.
- To encourage oral fluency start a discussion. Sometimes friends like different things. Is it okay to like different things? "I like to sit in the sun. Do you like to sit in the sun or in the shade?" "I like peanut butter sandwiches better than cheese sandwiches. Which do you like best?"

Klise, Kate. *Imagine Harry.* Harcourt, 2007.

After Little Rabbit starts school, he sees less and less of his invisible friend, Harry, and finally tells his mother that Harry moved away.

Literacy Features: Narrative skill, print awareness

Extended Learning Activities:

- Let's imagine Harry. Ask the children to describe Harry. You may need to ask questions such as, does he have long ears? Is he tall or short? Draw him on the white board. It is okay for the drawing to be primitive. The children will enjoy seeing your drawing.
- Write *Imagine Harry* on the white board in cursive (as it is written on the book cover) and in print lettering. Show that both types of writing mean the same.

Sample Storytime Plan

Theme: Friends—a friend is someone who likes you

Presentation Dates: _____

Literacy Skill Focus: Narrative skill

Books:

  A Friend for Minerva Louise by Janet Stoeke
  Imagine Harry by Kate Klise

Extended Learning Activities:

- Retell the story of *A Friend for Minerva Louise* by pointing to the picture of each object she finds. What does Minerva think this is? What do you think it is?
- Describe Little Rabbit's friend, Harry. Give the children paper and crayons. Draw a picture of Harry.

Songs, Rhymes, and Rhyming Stories:

  Opening: Time for Storytime (p. 47)

  Two Best Friends (p. 78)
  Jack and Jill (p. 52)
  Storytime Dance (p. 46)

  Closing: Goodbye for Now (p. 38)

Handouts:

  Two Best Friends finger puppets (p. 79)

GET DRESSED

Introduction

We express ourselves through the clothes we wear. You may have a collection of hats, a wedding dress, a work uniform or some sports clothes to show. These real items will be interesting to your group. Bring books with pictures of traditional costumes from a variety of cultures. Ask questions as you show them to your storytime group to generate a conversation about the clothes they like to wear. Maybe one or two of the storytime participants will stand up and show what they are wearing. This storytime is excellent for learning and practicing the vocabulary of clothing, and for encouraging oral fluency as the group talks about the clothes they like.

Books to Share with Extended Learning Activities

Barkow, Henriette. *If Elephants Wore Pants . . .* Sterling, 2004.

As a child is falling asleep, he begins to dream about an elephant who wears a different pair of pants for everything he does. He has fluffy pink pants for playing in the yard, and pants covered in stars for looking through a telescope.

Literacy Features: Phonological awareness, narrative skill

Extended Learning Activities:

- Select a few pairs of rhymes from the book and ask the children to think of additional rhyming words for the pair. For example: sun and fun rhyme with one, done, bun. To encourage participation you may ask each parent and child couple to think of one pair of rhyming words.
- Practice narrative skill by asking the children to recall what kind of pants the elephant wore in the woods, at the circus, etc.

Arnold, Ted. *Huggly Gets Dressed.* Scholastic, 1999.

Huggly, a little monster who lives under a child's bed, tries on the child's clothes. Without knowing the way people wear them, he puts them on in his own unique way.

Literacy Features: Vocabulary, narrative skill

Extended Learning Activities:

- Reinforce vocabulary and oral fluency with this activity. Bring some child-sized clothes and a teddy bear or other toy animal. Ask the children questions such as, "Shall I put these socks on his hands?" "Does the T-shirt go on the top or the bottom?" You may ask one of the parents to repeat the activity so they can practice asking questions, also.
- Make up new words to the song "Put your finger in the air." For example:
    Put your finger on your shirt, on your shirt.
    Put your finger on your shirt, on your shirt.
    Put your finger on your shirt. Oh no! I see some dirt.
    Put your finger on your shirt, on your shirt.

(Put your finger on your pants. Now get up and do a dance.)
(Put your finger on your shoe. I am very proud of you.)

Rollings, Susan. *New Shoes Red Shoes*. Orchard, 2001.

On a shopping trip with her mother a little girl sees many kinds of shoes, and finally finds the perfect pair of shoes for her.

Literacy Features: Vocabulary, narrative skill

Extended Learning Activities:

- Bring in a variety of shoes. Play show-and-tell with the shoes, giving their name and purpose. For example: "These are booties. They keep the baby's feet warm. These are high-heel shoes. Ladies wear them when they dress up."
- Go on a pretend shoe shopping trip. Pantomime trying on hiking boots, bedroom slippers, flip-flops, tap dancing shoes, shoes that tie, and shoes that close with Velcro.

Chodos-Irvine, Margaret. *Ella Sarah Gets Dressed*. Harcourt, 2003.

Ella Sarah gets dressed and puts on the clothes she prefers, which are not the ones suggested by her father, mother, or sister. She thinks her outfit is just right, and so do her creatively dressed friends.

Literacy Features: Vocabulary, print motivation, narrative skill

Extended Learning Activities:

- Ask the parents to tell the group about one of their child's favorite outfits or item of clothing.

Sample Storytime Plan

Theme: Get Dressed—expressing ourselves through the clothes we wear

Presentation Dates: _____

Literacy Skill Focus: Vocabulary

Books:

New Shoes Red Shoes by Susan Rollings
Ella Sarah Gets Dressed by Margaret Chodos-Irvine

Extended Learning Activities:

- Dressing a teddy bear in baby clothes
- Shoes show-and-tell
- Flash cards activity:
    Pass out picture flash cards for clothing vocabulary such as pants, shirt, dress, shoes, socks, skirt, coat, hat, belt
    Ask the children to bring them up one at a time and say the word as they give it to you.
    Prop three flash cards on the table or white board. Ask everyone to close their eyes. Take away one picture. Ask them to open their eyes and name the one that is missing.

Songs, Rhymes, and Rhyming Stories:

Opening: Time for Storytime (p. 47)

Teddy Bear, Teddy Bear (p. 64)
The Tabby Cat (p. 84)
Raise Them High (p. 44)

Closing: Goodbye for Now (p. 38)

Handouts:

Teddy Bear, Teddy Bear rhyme and coloring page (p. 64)

HATS OFF!

Introduction

There is something fascinating about hats! From ladies' dress hats with ribbons and flowers, to working hats for firemen and cowboys, hats are fabulous accessories. You can introduce this storytime with a dressing-up game. Bring in a variety of hats for the group. Stand everyone in a line, count to three, and then everyone passes their hat to the person on their right. The last person runs to the head of the line to give the first person his hat.

Books to Share with Extended Learning Activities:

Low, Alice. *Aunt Lucy Went to Buy a Hat.* HarperCollins, 2004.

Aunt Lucy sets out to buy a hat, but instead she buys a cat. It is just so easy to get sidetracked by all the lovely shops.

Literacy Features: Phonological awareness, vocabulary

Extended Learning Activities:

- Look for Aunt Lucy's hat hidden somewhere on each spread.
- What would Aunt Lucy buy? Extend the experience by asking children to name something Aunt Lucy would buy. This is an exercise for vocabulary and phonological awareness (rhyme). For example, if Aunt Lucy went out to buy a coat, what might she buy? (a goat or a boat). If she went out to buy some pears she might return with (chairs or stairs).

Willard, Nancy. *Mouse, the Cat, and Grandmother's Hat.* Little, Brown, 2003.

This rhyming story tells the tale of events that befall a family after a mouse hides under the grandmother's birthday hat.

Literacy Features: Phonological awareness, letter knowledge

Extended Learning Activities:

- What rhymes with hat? Cat, sat, that, mat, bat
- Write the words on the white board
- Point to the letter M on the cover. Draw the letter M in the air with your finger.

Rumford, James. *Don't Touch My Hat.* Knopf, 2007.

A sheriff in the old West keeps his town, Sunshine, free of crime while wearing his ten-gallon hat.

Literacy Features: Narrative skill, vocabulary

Extended Learning Activities:

- Use pictures or real workers' hats such as a cowboy hat, a fireman hat, a hard hat, a chef's hat, etc. Ask the children, "Who wears this hat to work?"
- Play the game Don't Touch My Hat: Blow up a balloon and put a hat on it. Pass the balloon from person to person without touching the hat or letting it drop to the floor.

Moore, Lilian. *While You Were Chasing a Hat.* **HarperFestival, 2001.**

The wind that whirled your hat away also filled the sails on a boat, tugged at a kite, and shook the trees.

Literacy Features: Vocabulary, letter knowledge

Extended Learning Activities:

- Narrative skill through pantomime: While making a wind sound (oooo!) coach the children in pantomiming the activities of the wind in this story. You may include blowing a hat off of someone's head, pushing the sails of a boat, tugging at a kite, riding the waves on the sea, etc. Expand this activity to include blowing bubbles, drying the laundry, blowing dry leaves in the fall, or other windy fun.
- Write the word WIND on the white board. Show that the first letter is W. Demonstrate that the sound of W is like a puff of wind.

Sample Storytime Plan

Theme: Hats Off!—hats as fabulous accessories

Presentation Dates: _____

Literacy Skill Focus: Phonological awareness

Books:

> *While You Were Chasing a Hat* by Lilian Moore
> *Mouse, the Cat, and Grandmother's Hat* by Nancy Willard

Extended Learning Activities:

- Make the sound of the wind and the sound of letter W.
- What rhymes with hat? Cat, sat, that, mat, bat.
- Write the rhyming words on the white board.
- Game: Hats on, Hats off!
    Form a circle.
    Give everyone a hat or cap to wear.
    Play recorded music while everyone walks around the circle.
    Turn off the music; have all stop and take off their hats and shout "Hats off!"

Songs, Rhymes, and Rhyming Stories:

Opening: Time for Storytime (p. 47)

W Is Lots of Fun (p. 49)
Raise Them High (p. 44)
The Wind, the Sun, and the Whistling Traveler (p. 88)

Closing: Goodbye for Now (p. 38)

Handouts:

Story and pattern for the Wind, the Sun, and the Whistling Traveler (pp. 88-89)

JUST THE RIGHT SIZE

Introduction

Introduce the concept of size with one or more of these activities:

- Show three toy balls of various sizes and three similar-sized boxes. Ask the storytime group to tell you which box is just the right size for each ball.
- Show a key ring with several sizes of keys on it. Talk about locks on doors, cars, bike locks, and padlocks. It takes a key that is just the right size to open a lock.
- Ask two people to take off a shoe, and then ask them to try on the other person's shoe. It does not fit. Your shoe has to be just the right size for your foot.

Books to Share with Extended Learning Activities

Roddie, Shen. *You're Too Small.* Tiger Tales, 2004.

Tad wants to help with the chores on the farm, but everyone thinks he is too small. When they get locked out of the barn, however, Tad says "I can help!"

Literacy Features: Vocabulary, narrative skill

Extended Learning Activities:

- Vocabulary size words matching game: Bring some bowls of various sizes to storytime. After reading *You're Too Small,* ask the children to sort the bowls into three groups: Small, medium, and large.
- Narrative skill: See if the children can name the various animals from this book, and also name the job they were doing (pig pushing a wheelbarrow, goat stacking hay, etc.). Let them try it from memory, and then turn the pages of the book again to take another look.

Minters, Frances. *Too Big, Too Small, Just Right.* Harcourt, 2001.

A bunny couple and their tiny mouse friend experience many funny encounters while shopping for bikes, dancing, camping, and skating in this charming exploration of opposites.

Literacy Features: Vocabulary, print motivation

Extended Learning Activities:

- Opposites vocabulary activity: Ask the children to name the opposite words as you turn the pages again (big and small, short and tall, dark and bright, etc.). Now explore some more opposites that you and the children can think of.
- Name something that you would like to have "many" of (shoes, puppies, friends, etc.). Name something that you would like to have "few" of (ice cubes in my glass, pickles on my sandwich, bows in my hair, etc.).

Dunbar, Joyce. *The Very Small.* Harcourt, 2000.

Giant Baby Bear finds a "very small . . . something" and he offers to share his mommy and daddy, his toys and his dinner until he can help the "very small" go home.

Literacy Features: Print motivation

Extended Learning Activities:

- Make a playground for your own "very small" using building blocks, cardboard tubes, kitchen tools, and other household items.
- Sing a lullaby that might help the "very small" fall asleep.

Weeks, Sarah. *Mrs. McNosh and the Great Big Squash.* HarperFestival, 2000.

Mrs. McNosh plants a squash seed in her garden and right away it starts to grow. Soon a huge squash is crashing and smashing the neighborhood. What is she going to do?

Literacy Features: Narrative skill, print motivation

Extended Learning Activities:

- Ask the children to think of some funny things that may happen when a vegetable in the garden grows to giant size. (It could grow bigger than the car, it could knock a bird's nest out of a tree, etc.)
- Start an imagination discussion. Mrs. McNosh made a house out of her squash. What would you like to make a house out of? (Build a house out of snow, build a house out of glue and feathers, build a house out of candy, etc.)

Sample Storytime Plan

Theme: Just the Right Size—the concept of small, medium, and large

Presentation Dates: _____

Literacy Skill Focus: Narrative skill

Books:

Mrs. McNosh and the Great Big Squash by Sarah Weeks
You're Too Small by Roddie Shen

Extended Learning Activities:

- Start an imagination discussion. Mrs. McNosh made a house out of her squash. What would you like to make a house out of? (Build a house out of snow, build a house out of glue and feathers, build a house out of candy, etc.)
- Make houses out of blocks, or use Sparkling Snow Play Dough (see Appendix) to form houses.
- Name the various animals from *You're Too Small* and name the job they were doing (pig pushing a wheelbarrow, goat stacking hay, etc.).
- Patterned sentences to write on the white board:

   A mouse is small.
   A bird is small.
   An apple is small.
   A horse is big.
   A fire truck is big.
   A tree is big.

Songs, Rhymes, and Rhyming Stories:

Opening: Time for Storytime (p. 47)

There Was an Old Woman Who Lived in a Shoe (p. 57)
I'm a Little Teapot (p. 66)
Raise Them High (p. 44)

Closing: Goodbye for Now (p. 38)

Handouts:

Recipe for Sparkling Snow Play Dough (see Appendix)

MY FEELINGS

Introduction

Introduce this theme by giving several scenarios. Use vocal inflection and facial features to emphasize the emotion of the scenario. After each scenario, ask your Family Literacy Storytime group "How did you feel?" You may ask one or two adults from your group to tell a scenario for everyone to guess.

For example: On a really hot day last week I went to the store to buy a cool and yummy ice cream cone. I asked for two scoops of my favorite flavor, strawberry. "We don't have strawberry ice cream today," the man said. How did I feel?

Books to Share with Extended Learning Activities

Dewdney, Anna. *Llama Llama Mad at Mama*. Viking, 2007.

When Llama Llama has to interrupt his playtime to go shopping with Mama, he can only take it for so long. And then, he gets mad!

Literacy Features: Vocabulary, phonological awareness, letter knowledge

Extended Learning Activities:

- Vocabulary: Shop-o-rama game. Find food flash cards or cut out pictures from food ads for some common food items to shop for. Distribute them to the children. Call out the name of an item and have the child holding that picture come up and put it in the shopping basket. Repeat until all of the items have been collected.
- Phonological awareness and letter knowledge: Pretend you are shopping for things that start with the "B" sound. How many can the children think of? (bananas, bread, bagels, beets, butter, biscuits, beef, etc.) Write their suggestions on a white board. Point to the letter "b" in each word. You may repeat, choosing a different beginning letter sound.

Juster, Norton. *The Hello Good-bye Window*. Hyperion, 2005.

A little girl describes her day with Nanna and Poppy in their big house with a picture window. From this window she sees her parents coming to pick her up. The little girl feels happy and sad at the same time. She is happy to see them but sad that her visit with Nanna and Poppy will end.

Literacy Features: Narrative skill, print motivation

Extended Learning Activities:

- In this story Poppy plays the harmonica in a lot of different ways. Slow or fast, sitting down or standing up. Sing "Row, Row, Row Your Boat" (or another song) with the children several different ways.
- Ask questions to encourage oral fluency and narrative skill. What makes you happy? What makes you sad? Can you be happy and sad at the same time?

Chodos-Irvine, Margaret. *Best Best Friends.* Harcourt, 2006.

Even best best friends who always sit together at storytime get mad sometimes. "You're not nice!" Mary tells Clare. "You're not, either!" Clare tells Mary. But after naptime, a little gift and some building blocks change their feelings.

Literacy Features: Narrative skill, print motivation

Extended Learning Activities:

- Color fun: Looking for pink. Look at each illustration again, and ask the children to find something pink on the page. For example, pink dots on the teddy bear's ribbon, pink puzzle pieces, pink socks, pink shoes, and pink cupcakes. Then look again for green, brown, yellow, etc.
- Counting: Count the number of children on the storytime page, the lining up page and the party page.

Bailey, Linda. *Goodnight, Sweet Pig.* Kids Can, 2007.

A little pig cannot get to sleep one night because the other pigs are so loud. Pigs playing music! Pigs playing ball! When she begins to cry, the other pigs feel sorry. (Pigs are nicer than they look.)

Literacy Features: Vocabulary, narrative skill

Extended Learning Activities:

- Narrative skill: Ask the children about their bedtime. Do they want a story or a song at bedtime? Do they want all the lights off or do they like a night-light?
- Vocabulary: Reinforce understanding of verbs. Play an action game based on activities in the book. Ask the children to pantomime these actions:

    Eat some toast
    Paint your trotters (toes)
    Juggle some plums
    Ride your pony
    Beat your drums
    Step in the cake
    Bounce your ball
    Wipe a tear
    Tiptoe quietly
    Close your eyes

Sample Storytime Plan

Theme: My Feelings—talking about emotions

Presentation Dates: _____

Literacy Skill Focus: Vocabulary

Books:

Llama Llama Mad at Mama by Anna Dewdney
Goodnight, Sweet Pig by Linda Bailey

Extended Learning Activities:
- Shop-o-rama game with food flash cards
- Pantomime these actions:

> *Eat* some toast
> *Paint* your trotters (toes)
> *Juggle* some plums
> *Ride* your pony
> *Beat* your drums
> *Step* in the cake
> *Bounce* your ball
> *Wipe* a tear
> *Tiptoe* quietly
> *Close* your eyes

Songs, Rhymes, and Rhyming Stories:

Opening: Time for Storytime (p. 47)

Happy Puppy (p. 82)
Raise Them High (p. 44)
Would You Like to Fly? (p. 50)
Here Is the Church (p. 65)

Closing: Goodbye for Now (p. 38)

Handouts:

Happy Puppy coloring sheet (p. 83)

NANCY TAFURI NATURE WALKS

Introduction

Author Nancy Tafuri includes animals and the natural world in her books. Introduce the storytime by taking a pretend walk to the woods, to the sea, or to the lake. What do you hear? What kind of animals do you see? Is the day sunny and warm, or breezy, or chilly?

Books to Share with Extended Learning Activities

Tafuri, Nancy. *Whose Chick Are You?* Greenwillow, 2007.

A chick hatches out of an egg. Does it belong to Goose, Duck, Hen, Bird, or Swan?

Literacy Features: Vocabulary, print awareness

Extended Learning Activities:

- Turn the pages a second time and ask the children to name the birds on the page and make their sound.
- What is a baby duck called? What is a baby chicken called? What is a baby goose called? A baby swan is called a cygnet.

Tafuri, Nancy. *The Busy Little Squirrel.* Simon & Schuster, 2007.

A busy squirrel is trying to get ready for winter, but his friends want him to play.

Literacy Features: Print awareness, vocabulary

Extended Learning Activities:

- Point to the text and show that reading in English goes from left to right. Each time you come to the word squirrel, point to it. Then ask a child to point to the word squirrel.
- Vocabulary: Ask the children to stand and do the actions that busy little squirrel's friends suggest, such as hop on rocks and run in the field. Emphasize the meaning of the verbs.

Tafuri, Nancy. *Silly Little Goose.* Scholastic, 2001.

Goose is looking for a warm, cozy, soft place to build a nest, but the pig, the cat and the sheep don't like her choice. Finally goose finds a perfect place and hatches a surprise for everyone.

Literacy Features: Print motivation, print awareness

Extended Learning Activities:

- Because the type face is large, this book is good for developing print awareness. Show that words are read from left to right by pointing to the words as you read.
- Encourage the children to repeat the phrase "Silly Little Goose" as you read the book.

Tafuri, Nancy. *Where Did Bunny Go?* Scholastic, 2001.

On a snowy day, Bunny and Bird are playing hide and seek with their animal friends but Bird cannot find Bunny anywhere. Did Bunny run away?

Literacy Features: Narrative skill, print awareness

Extended Learning Activities:

- Most of the pages of this book are read holding the book "landscape" format. But when Bunny and Bird hop and roll in the new snow the book must be turned to "portrait" format. This is a good opportunity to show that words convey the meaning of the story, not just the pictures. Point to the words as you read.
- Encourage narrative skill by asking, "When they played hide and seek, who did Bird find first? Where did she find him? Who did Bird find last? Where was he hiding?"

Sample Storytime Plan

Theme: Nancy Tafuri Nature Walks—exploring the natural world

Presentation Dates: _____

Literacy Skill Focus: Print awareness

Books:

The Busy Little Squirrel by Nancy Tafuri
Where Did Bunny Go? by Nancy Tafuri

Extended Learning Activities:

- Point to the text and show that reading in English goes from left to right.
- Look for the word Bunny and ask a child to point to it.
- Go on a pretend nature walk on a snowy day. First, pantomime putting on boots, hats and coats. Now narrate the walk with activities such as crunching through the deep snow, rolling a snowball, looking for Bunny under the tree, looking for Bird flying overhead, etc.
- Ask: "What will you do on your nature walk today?" Write answers on white board.
    I will hop on rocks.
    I will run in the field.
    I will throw a snowball.
    I will find a pinecone.
    I will hear a bird sing.
    I will jump in a puddle.

Songs, Rhymes, and Rhyming Stories:

Opening: Time for Storytime (p. 47)

Leaves Are Falling (p. 39)
Two Little Black Birds (p. 62)
Singing Tonight (p. 74)

Closing: Goodbye for Now (p. 38)

Handouts:

Singing Tonight rhyming story and color page (pp. 74-75)

OH, BABY!

Introduction

Bring a baby doll to storytime. Be sure to have a blanket, bottle, toys, and other baby needs. Ask the storytime group to name the objects and explain how they are used to help baby. Even though they are big now, once they were very tiny and helpless.

Books to Share with Extended Learning Activities

Meyers, Susan. *This Is the Way the Baby Rides.* Abrams, 2005.

While Mommy, Daddy, and baby have a summer picnic, animal families enjoy similar activities such as running, hiding, eating, and playing.

Literacy Features: Vocabulary, phonological awareness

Extended Learning Activities:

- Turn the pages a second time and talk about the activities each animal family is doing. Ask the children to repeat the sounds of the activities (quick-ity quick, bounce-ity bounce, etc.). This activity will reinforce phonological awareness.
- For vocabulary building, ask the children to name each animal family (rabbits, foxes, otters, ducks, etc.).

Clerk, Jessica. *Wriggly, Wriggly Baby.* Levine, 2002.

In this funny tall tale, a very active baby wriggles away from home and goes to the firehouse, the zoo, the diner and finally back home to his parents.

Literacy Features: Letter knowledge, phonological awareness

Extended Learning Activities:

- Phonological awareness: Point out some of the alliteration in the story (tangoed with the tigers, babbled with the bears). Ask "What else can the baby do with the tiger that begins with the T sound?" Suggest tickle, tap dance, talk, trip, etc. Write the suggestions on the white board.
- The baby's dog and cat help him through his journey. See if the children can find the pets on each page. Ask them to describe what the dog and cat are doing.

Henderson, Kathy. *Baby Knows Best.* Little, Brown, 2002.

Everybody wants to make baby happy. Baby has lots of toys and games, but chooses to play with ordinary household things.

Literacy Features: Vocabulary, letter knowledge

Extended Learning Activities:

- Ask the children to name something that a baby needs. Ask them to tell why the baby needs it or how baby uses it.
- Play a game to reinforce the letter sound B. Each person makes a statement such as "I am a baby and I want a banana (ball, blanket, boat, bear, binky, etc.)." See how many B words the group can name.

Smith, Maggie. *One Naked Baby*. Knopf, 2007.

A full day of activities for a baby including playing indoors and outdoors, beginning and ending with one naked baby in the bath.

Literacy Features: Vocabulary, print awareness

Extended Learning Activities:

- For oral fluency and vocabulary practice, ask questions about the objects found on each page of the book. For example, "What color is the toy truck? What is the baby having for a snack? What kind of animal is this?"
- Print awareness: Point to the numbers on the sidebar of each page. Show the number word written in bold text on the page. Count the objects on the page.

Sample Storytime Plan

Theme: Oh, Baby!—once we were all very tiny and helpless

Presentation Dates: _____

Literacy Skill Focus: Phonological awareness

Books:

This Is the Way the Baby Rides by Susan Meyers
Baby Knows Best by Kathy Henderson

Extended Learning Activities:

- When reading *This Is the Way the Baby Rides,* repeat the sounds of the activities (quick-ity quick, bounce-ity bounce, etc.)
- List some things on the white board that baby wants that start with the "B" sound. Each person makes a statement such as "I am a baby and I want a banana (ball, blanket, boat, bear, binky, etc.)."
- Discussion: What are some things that baby needs? Why does baby need it?

Songs, Rhymes, and Rhyming Stories:

Opening: Time for Storytime (p. 47)

Five Baby Dragons (p. 70)
Family (p. 37)
Storytime Dance (p. 46)

Closing: Goodbye for Now (p. 38)

Handouts:

Five Baby Dragons story and pictures (pp. 70–71) or Bathtub Paint recipe (see Appendix)

OH BROTHER, OH SISTER!

Introduction

Show a picture of your brother or sister and tell a funny story from your childhood memories. Ask your storytime group to tell the names of their brothers and sisters.

Books to Share with Extended Learning Activities

Pham, Leuyen. *Big Sister, Little Sister.* Hyperion, 2005.

Big sister gets new clothes, likes to try on lipstick, and isn't afraid of the dark. Little sister is always trying to catch up to her big sister, but she is good at lots of things, too.

Literacy Features: Vocabulary, narrative skill

Extended Learning Activities:

- Opposites: After reading the book, talk about big and little. Use picture cards, toys or realia to illustrate.
- In this book Big Sister tells good stories. Work on narrative skill by creating a story together such as: "Once upon a time there was a big dragon. He lived in a house on the top of the hill. One day he went out to play. The dragon went skipping along the path. Ooops! He tripped over his big feet and went rolling, rolling, rolling down the hill. Splash! The dragon fell into the stream. "Hurray!" shouted the dragon! "That was fun."

Fitzpatrick, Marie-Louise. *Silly Mommy, Silly Daddy.* Francis Lincoln, 2007.

Beth will not smile today. Mommy and Daddy try their best to cheer her up but she just thinks they are sillybillies. When big sister comes home and sticks out her tongue, Beth might just have to crack a smile after all.

Literacy Features: Print motivation, phonological awareness

Extended Learning Activities:

- Play with the funny sounds in the book such as "Eatums, eatums, yum, yum, yum." Say it over and over while the children spoon imaginary pudding into their mouths.
- Also try repeating "Clip-clop, clip-clop, clip-clop" while the children run in place.

Vestergaard, Hope. *What Do You Do When a Monster Says Boo?* Dutton, 2006.

When a little sister throws tantrums, pulls hair, or feels blue, big brother knows just what to do.

Literacy Features: Vocabulary, letter knowledge

Extended Learning Activities:

- Vocabulary building fun with synonyms: Review some of the "monstrous" behavior in the book (holler, howl, throw, grab, pull). Ask the children to think of another word that means the same: holler = yell; howl = cry; throw = toss; grab = snatch; pull = tug.
- Color fun and letter recognition: Each letter in the word MONSTER on the cover and title page is written in a different color. Name the letters and name the colors.

Shea, Pegi Deitz. *New Moon*. Boyds Mills, 2000.

When Vinnie's big brother shows her the full moon through the window, she begins looking for moons in nursery rhymes and picture books. There is no moon in the sky for some time after that, but one afternoon her big brother rushes home from school to show her that the moon has come out to play with her in the daylight.

Literacy Features: Print motivation, narrative skills

Extended Learning Activities:

- Recite the rhyme "Hey Diddle Diddle." Put a moon shape on the floor, and let the children take turns jumping over it.
- Show pictures of the moon in various phases. Show the children how the moon looks like an O sometimes, and sometimes it looks like a D or backward D.

Mitton, Tony. *Goodnight Me, Goodnight You*. Little, Brown, 2002.

At bedtime a brother and sister say goodnight to everything in their world, including airplanes, animals, their own toys, and finally to each other.

Literacy Features: Vocabulary, letter knowledge, print motivation

Extended Learning Activities:

- Discuss examples from the book about where animals sleep. For example: birds sleep in a nest, rabbits sleep in burrows, sheep sleep in the field, the cat sleeps on the bed.
- Look for the uppercase G on each page of the book.

Sample Storytime Plan

Theme: Oh Brother, Oh Sister!—fun we share with our siblings

Presentation Dates: _____

Literacy Skill Focus: Print motivation

Books:

> *Silly Mommy, Silly Daddy* by Marie-Louise Fitzpatrick
> *What Do You Do When a Monster Says Boo?* by Hope Vetergaard

Extended Learning Activities:

- Print motivation is about enjoyment of books. Be spontaneous and playful while reading.
- Play with the funny sounds in *Silly Mommy, Silly Daddy* such as "Eatums, eatums, yum, yum, yum." Say it over and over while the children spoon imaginary pudding into their mouths.
- Also try repeating "Clip-clop, clip-clop, clip-clop" while the children run in place.
- Color fun and letter recognition: Each letter in the word MONSTER on the cover and title page is written in a different color. Name the letters and name the colors.
- Game: Oh Brother, Oh Sister. Pass a beanbag around the room as quickly as you can. If it drops, everyone calls out, "Oh, Brother, Oh, Sister." Then the play resumes until everyone is giggling. For extra fun, pass more than one beanbag.

Songs, Rhymes, and Rhyming Stories:

Opening: Time for Storytime (p. 47)

Humpty Dumpty (p. 59)
Family (p. 37)
Jack Be Nimble (p. 55)

Closing: Goodbye for Now (p. 38)

Handouts:

Humpty Dumpty rhyme and coloring page (p. 59)

PEEP, HONK, QUACK

Introduction

Show photos of a chick, a goose, and a duck. Discuss how these three birds are similar and how they are different. Teach them that a chick says "peep," a goose says "honk," and a duck says "quack."

Books to Share with Extended Learning Activities

Anastas, Margaret. *A Hug for You*. HarperCollins, 2005.

There are many hugs for a duckling during the day spent with friends. Hugs are for "a cold winter day, to chase monsters away, for getting so tall, for no reason at all." The best hug of all comes at the end of the day when duckling hugs its parent.

Literacy Features: Print motivation, phonological awareness

Extended Learning Activities:

- Let the children name the duckling's friends as you turn the pages for a second time (dragonfly, mouse, fish, etc.).
- Choose a few of the rhyming pairs, and encourage the group to think of another word that rhymes with them. Day, away and play. Tall, all and wall. Write them on the white board.

Mallat, Kathy. *Just Ducky*. Walker, 2004.

Ducky quacks and squawks calling various friends to play, but they are too busy. He finally finds a little, yellow, fuzzy creature who seems just right for a playmate.

Literacy Features: Letter knowledge, phonological awareness, narrative skill

Extended Learning Activities:

- Write the phrase "Bee is too busy bizz-buzzing away" on the white board. Ask a few children to come up and point to a letter "B." Show both the uppercase and lowercase "B." Think of more words that begin with the same sound.
- Large motor skills fun: Ask the children to pantomime the actions as you ask questions based on the book. Encourage jumping or running in place by demonstrating for them. "Can you hip-hop away like Frog? Can you dash-dart away like Mouse? Can you spin all around like Ducky?"

Hills, Tad. *Duck and Goose*. Schwartz and Wade, 2006.

Duck and Goose mistake a big ball for an egg, and fight over taking care of it. They spend hours sitting together on top of it to keep it warm. Eventually they learn that it isn't really an egg, but by then a friendship has formed between them.

Literacy Features: Narrative skill, print awareness

Extended Learning Activities:

- Bring a large playground ball and let two children try to sit on it together like Duck and Goose. Retell the story as a group while the two children act out the story.

- For large motor skills, play "catch the egg" with a playground ball.
- Counting activity: Try one of these ideas to reinforce number knowledge. Make 10 duck shapes and count them as you put them on the magnet or flannel board. Float some bathtub ducks in a small pan, counting them together as you do. Touch the children on the head and count saying, "One duck, two ducks, three ducks, etc."

Stenmark, Victoria. *The Singing Chick.* Holt, 1999.

A newly hatched, happily singing chick is eaten by a fox, who then starts singing before being eaten by a wolf, and so begins a chain of eating and singing for a series of animals.

Literacy Features: Narrative skill, phonological awareness

Extended Learning Activities:

- Read the singing chick's song again, pausing to let the children complete each phrase. "The sky is so . . . (blue). The sun is so . . . (yellow).
- To reinforce narrative skills, ask leading questions so the children can retell the story. The chick was swallowed by a . . . ? The fox was swallowed by a . . . ? The wolf was swallowed by a . . . ?

Sample Storytime Plan

Theme: Peep, Honk, Quack—stories about chicks, geese, and ducks

Presentation Dates: _____

Literacy Skill Focus: Narrative skill

Books:

Duck and Goose by Tad Hills
The Singing Chick by Victoria Stenmark

Extended Learning Activities:

- Retell the stories through pantomime and questioning
- White board activity: Rhyming
    Chick quick brick
    Duck truck luck
    Goose moose loose
- Narrative activity: Create a short story from the rhyming words on the white board. For example:
    Once there was a little chick. He was very quick. When he saw a falling brick he ran away!
    One day a duck crossed the road. He did not see the truck that was coming. He saw a pretty rock on the other side of the road. He ran to get it. What luck! The truck did not hit him.

Songs, Rhymes, and Rhyming Stories:

Opening: Time for Storytime (p. 47)

Someday I Would (p. 45)
Humpty Dumpty (p. 59)

Way Up in the Apple Tree (p. 67)

Closing: Goodbye for Now (p. 38)

Handouts:

Humpty Dumpty rhyme and coloring page (p. 59)

PUPPIES

Introduction

A puppy is so appealing! A puppy is soft, cute, playful, and loving. But a puppy takes a lot of care. This storytime theme may generate conversations about being helpful, doing your chores, and taking care of pets. You may want to bring a dish and some puppy food so children can practice pouring.

Books to Share with Learning Activities

Lee, Spike. *Please, Puppy, Please.* Simon & Schuster, 2005.

Two children teach their puppy about bath time, the cat, and coming when they call.

Literacy Features: Vocabulary, letter knowledge

Extended Learning Activities:

- Turn the pages again and help the children find the letter P, which occurs frequently through the book.
- Narrative skill: Lead the children and parents in a discussion about how to keep a puppy safe and happy by playing carefully, patting him gently, keeping the gate closed, and throwing a ball for him.

Thayer, Jane. *The Puppy Who Wanted a Boy.* HarperCollins, 2003.

A new edition of a classic picture book, with updated text and illustrations. Petey, a puppy, wanted a boy for Christmas more than anything in the world. He didn't expect to find so many boys who wanted to offer him a home.

Literacy Features: Narrative skill, print motivation

Extended Learning Activities:

- Game: Pass the puppy. Use a stuffed toy puppy. Play some music and have the children pass the toy from child to child until the music stops. The child holding the puppy toy brings him to you so the game can be repeated.

Lewis, Kim. *Little Puppy.* Candlewick, 2000.

On Katie's farm a bundle of five black and white Border collie puppies have just arrived. She carefully holds and strokes one of the puppies while the mother dog watches close by. The simple text and pastel illustrations invite children to experience the pastoral setting.

Literacy Features: Print awareness, vocabulary

Extended Learning Activities:

- Counting activity: Using flannel or magnet board figures of five puppies, practice counting to five.
- Letter knowledge: Use magnetic letters or a white board and markers to spell puppy and let the children identify and say the letters out loud.

Thayer, Jane. *Part-time Dog.* HarperCollins, 2004.

Three neighbors share the care of a little brown dog, although none of them wants a dog. After Brownie spends a night in the dog pound, however, they agree to share responsibility for him and rescue him from the pound. This reissue of a 1965 book has cute, bright illustrations.

Literacy Features: Narrative skill, vocabulary

Extended Learning Activities:

- Who is your neighbor? Ask each child in turn to name the child seated to his left and his right. Ask each adult to name one of the neighbors who lives near his or her home.

Sample Storytime Plan

Theme: Puppies—a puppy takes a lot of care

Presentation Dates: _____

Literacy Skill Focus: Letter knowledge

Books:

> *Please, Puppy, Please* by Spike Lee
> *Little Puppy* by Kim Lewis

Extended Learning Activities:

- Use magnetic letters to spell PUPPY on the white board. As you read each book, look for the letter P on the title page. Draw a letter P in the air with your finger. Select rhymes that include the letter P.
- Who is your neighbor? Ask each child in turn to name the child seated to his left and his right. Ask each adult to name one of the neighbors who lives near his or her home.
- Game: Pass the puppy. Use a stuffed toy puppy. Play some music and have the children pass the toy from child to child until the music stops. The child holding the puppy toy brings him to you so the game can be repeated.

Songs, Rhymes, and Rhyming Stories:

> *Opening:* Time for Storytime (p. 47)

> Hey Diddle Diddle (p. 54)
> Happy Puppy (p. 82)
> Raise Them High (p. 44)

> *Closing:* Goodbye for Now (p. 38)

Handouts:

> Happy Puppy action rhyme and color page (pp. 82–83)

ROSEMARY WELLS, ILLUSTRATOR

Introduction

Rosemary Wells has illustrated books for other authors, as well as books that she wrote. Show some examples of her art and talk about her style. Ask the group if anyone of them likes to draw pictures, too. When you draw and paint pictures for a book you are the illustrator. If you have a favorite character, tell the group why you like it best.

Books to Share with Extended Learning Activities

Williams, Garth. *Benjamin's Treasure.* HarperCollins, 2001.

Benjamin Pink went fishing one day, only to be caught in a rainstorm and stranded on a deserted island with a chest full of treasure. The Garth Williams story has been adapted for picture book format by Rosemary Wells, and the original black-and-white illustrations have been colored using the exact pallet of paints available to Garth Williams in the 1950s.

Literacy Features: Narrative skills, vocabulary

Extended Learning Activities:

- Synonyms: Explore some of the vocabulary in the book by suggesting synonyms. The children will most likely supply additional synonyms. For example: enormous (huge, gigantic, great). Buccaneers (pirates, crooks). Leapfrogging (jumping, hopping).
- Buying presents: Make a list of the presents the children would like to buy if they found a treasure. Write their list on the white board.

Here Comes Mother Goose, Illustrated by Rosemary Wells. Candlewick, 1999.

A collection of nursery rhymes with charming illustrations featuring rabbits, ducklings, cats, and guinea pigs.

Literacy Features: Phonological awareness, print motivation

Extended Learning Activities:

- Read "Jelly on a Plate" and act out the rhyme. Encourage the children to "wibble wobble" by wiggling their bodies. Encourage them to "frizzle, frazzle" by spinning around like a sausage in a pan. Encourage them to reach down and touch the floor, then rock the baby in their arms.
- Read "Donkey, Donkey, Old and Gray." Encourage the children to bray like a donkey.

Wells, Rosemary. *Noisy Nora.* Puffin, 2000 (new illustrations for Dial 1973 picture book).

Nora, who is the middle child, feels neglected by her family. So she makes noise to attract the attention of her parents.

Literacy Features: Phonological awareness, vocabulary

Extended Learning Activities:

- The phrase "Nora had to wait" occurs several times. Encourage predicting by pausing to allow the children to complete the phrase.

- Rhyming fun: Ask the children to give additional rhyming words for some of the rhyming pairs in the book.
  - Kate, wait (gate, late, date)
  - Door, floor (more, four, score)

Loesser, Frank. *I Love You! A Bushel & a Peck*. Illustrated by Rosemary Wells. HarperCollins, 2005.

Two flirty ducklings play together, call each other on the phone, and dance together on the farm as they fall in love.

Literacy Features: Phonological awareness, print motivation

Extended Learning Activities:

- Encourage the children to join in when you say or sing "Doodle oodle oddle, doodle oodle oddle, a-doodle oodle oodle ooo." They may even want to get up and dance for this part of the story.
- Name the farm objects as you turn the pages a second time (tractor, corn, pumpkins, apple barrel).

Sample Storytime Plan

Theme: Rosemary Wells, Illustrator—illustrator with a unique style

Presentation Dates: _____

Literacy Skill Focus: Phonological awareness

Books:

Noisy Nora by Rosemary Wells
I Love You! A Bushel & a Peck by Frank Loesser

Extended Learning Activities:

- Show several illustrations by Rosemary Wells and talk about her style.
- Rhyming fun: Ask the children to give additional rhyming words for some of the rhyming pairs in Noisy Nora.
  - Kate, wait (gate, late, date)
  - Door, floor (more, four, score)
- When reading *I Love You! A Bushel & a Peck* encourage the children to join in when you say or sing "Doodle oodle oddle, doodle oodle oddle, a-doodle oodle oodle ooo." They may even want to get up and dance for this part of the story.

Songs, Rhymes, and Rhyming Stories:

Opening: Time for Storytime (p. 47)

Mary, Mary Quite Contrary (p. 56)
Little Bo-Peep (p. 58)
Little Jack Horner (p. 61)

Closing: Goodbye for Now (p. 38)

Handouts:

Little Bo-Peep coloring page (p. 58)

SLEEPY TIME

Introduction

Allow the children to bring blankets and teddy bears to storytime, and even wear pajamas. Lead a discussion about sleeping. Everyone sleeps but not everyone sleeps the same way. Get everyone to yawn and stretch before reading your first book.

Books to Share with Extended Learning Activities

Anastas, Margaret. *Mommy's Best Kisses.* HarperCollins, 2003.

Zebra, otter, giraffe, and human mothers kiss their babies good night on their small hands, plump tummy, pink knees, and rosy cheeks.

Literacy Features: Vocabulary, print motivation

Extended Learning Activities:

- Learning animal names: Name the animals on each page and include a descriptive comment. "This is a giraffe mother and baby. Giraffes have long, long necks. This is a polar bear mother and baby. I like their soft white fur."
- Action and vocabulary-building activity: Show each page again and ask the children a corresponding question. "Where are your small hands? Where is your sweet neck?"

Bauer, Marion Dane. *Sleep, Little One. Sleep.* Simon & Schuster, 1999.

A father coaxes his child to snuggle close, lie still and let sleep come. Pastel paintings of mice, sheep, horses, polar bears, and a whale create an inviting dream.

Literacy Features: Vocabulary, print motivation, letter knowledge

Extended Learning Activities:

- Demonstrate the size relationship of the animals in the book with a yawning and stretching activity. Start with very small gestures and slowly increase in size as you yawn like a spider, a mouse, a robin, a puppy, a tortoise, a sheep, and so on until you are yawning like a whale!
- Letter recognition: Show the large first capital letter on each page and ask the children to identify it.

Schaefer, Carole Lexa. *Down in the Woods at Sleepytime.* Candlewick, 2000.

All the mamas in the woods struggle to get their little ones to settle down for the night, until Grandma Owl tells them a bedtime story.

Literacy Features: Vocabulary, phonological awareness

Extended Learning Activities:

- Play with letter sounds found in the book. For example, snuffle for snacks. More words that begin with the same sound include sneak, snake, snip, snarl, snore. You may also use the pair, deep down. More words that begin with the same sound include dust, dance, dot, daisy, dog, dish.

Kanevsky, Polly. *Sleepy Boy.* Atheneum, 2006.

After a busy day, a little boy finds it hard to fall asleep. Comforted by his father, he begins to relax as he remembers seeing the lions at the zoo.

Literacy Features: Narrative skill, print motivation

Extended Learning Activities:

- Narrative skill through pantomime: Ask the children to act out sleepy-time activities such as brushing your teeth, putting on pajamas, laying your head on the pillow, closing your eyes, breathing slowly, etc.
- Show the illustrations again and ask the children about their bedtime activities. "Do you sometimes put your feet where your head should be? Do you cuddle next to Daddy or Mommy to fall asleep?"

Sample Storytime Plan

Theme: Sleepy Time—everyone sleeps, but not everyone sleeps the same way

Presentation Dates: _____

Literacy Skill Focus: Letter knowledge

Books:

Sleep, Little One. Sleep by Marion Dane Bauer
Down in the Woods at Sleepytime by Carole Lexa Shaefer

Extended Learning Activities:

- Ask everyone to stand up. Form a line, and walk a curved "s" shape together. Now everyone can sit. Remind them that Stand and Sit start with the letter S.
- Show the large first capital letter on each page and ask the children to identify it.
- White board activity: Write the letter S on the white board. Write the names that start with S of anyone in the group.

Songs, Rhymes, and Rhyming Stories:

Opening: Time for Storytime (p. 47)

Singing Tonight (p. 74)
Teddy Bear, Teddy Bear Turn Around (p. 64)
Storytime Dance (p. 46)

Closing: Goodbye for Now (p. 38)

Handouts:

Singing Tonight coloring page (p. 75)

SNOWY DAY FUN

Introduction

There is something very cozy about a snowy day! For some of your Family Literacy Storytime group members, snow may be a new experience. Make a memory for them with your storytime activities today. Make some snowballs ahead of time, and store them in the freezer to share with the children at this storytime. Cut paper snowflakes to decorate your space. You may even want to simulate a fireplace with paper logs and flames or a stack of fireplace logs. Wear your snow boots and bring your scarf and mittens.

Books to Share and Extended Learning Activities

Milbourne, Anna. *The Snowy Day*. Usborne, 2005.

Several children experience a winter day and night, with thousands of pretty snowflakes dancing through the sky and settling on fields and rooftops. Some interesting facts are presented in the text about how snowflakes form and what animals do when it is cold.

Literacy Features: Vocabulary, letter knowledge

Extended Learning Activities:

- Discussion of science concepts: Talk about how animals keep warm when the weather is cold.
- Ask questions for comprehension: What happens when raindrops freeze? How many points does a snowflake have? What sound do you hear when you walk through the snow?
- Show the cover and point to the letter S and the letter D. Draw the letters in the air with your finger, and then guide the children drawing them on the carpet. The texture of the carpet will tickle a bit.

Plourde, Lynn. *Snow Day*. Simon & Schuster, 2001.

Two children wake up to find snow covering trees and bushes. They spend a wonderful day with books, dressing up, playing checkers, and making snacks as a family.

Literacy Features: Vocabulary, phonological awareness

Extended Learning Activities:

- Talk about what kinds of clothes you should put on before going out into the snow (cap, scarf, boots, mittens, long johns, etc.)
- Turn to the page with the text "Wooooo-ooooo! Wild whirling wind." Point to the letter "W." Say the words together, and enjoy making the sound of the wind.

Waddell, Martin. *Snow Bears*. Candlewick, 2003.

When three little bears play in the snow, they pretend to be snow bears and their mother goes along with the game.

Literacy Features: Narrative skill, letter knowledge

Extended Learning Activities:

- In this story, three little bear cubs played a game with their mother. They pretended to be snow bears. Ask the parents and children to describe a game they like to play together.
- Turn to the page where the snow bears are melting. Point to the word DRIP which occurs several times on the page. Ask the children to say each letter.

Laminack, Lester. *Snow Day*. Peachtree, 2007.

If it snows tonight, so much that the school buses and the teachers cannot go to school, it could be a snow day. A father and his children imagine the fun activities they could enjoy if they cannot go to school the next day.

Literacy Features: Narrative skill, vocabulary

Extended Learning Activities:

- Action and imagination activity: Pretend you are trudging through the snow. At first it is as deep as your ankles. Pick your feet up high. But the snow is falling fast! Now the snow is as deep as your knees so you must take giant steps to walk through the snow. Finally you are home, and just in time! The snow is as deep as your head! Open the door and go inside. Take off your hat, your mittens, your coat, and your boots. Now snuggle down with a blanket and take a sip of hot cocoa.
- Ask questions to encourage understanding and oral fluency. Do you know what a weatherman does? What does predict mean? Do you hope the weatherman predicts a sunny day, a rainy day, or a snowy day? What is the weather like today?

Sample Storytime Plan

Theme: Snowy Day Fun—snow may be a new experience

Presentation Dates: _____

Literacy Skill Focus: Vocabulary

Books:

Snow Day by Lynn Plourde
Snow Bears by Martin Waddell

Extended Learning Activities:

- Pretend you are eating a warm breakfast, such as applesauce pancakes, before going out into the cold weather.
- Vocabulary activity: Dress a teddy bear for going out in the snow with a scarf, some mittens, a hat, and a jacket. Try to put your snow boots on him. It will be funny that they do not fit.
- Action and imagination activity: Pretend you are trudging through the snow. At first it is as deep as your ankles. Pick your feet up high. But the snow is falling fast! Now the snow is as deep as your knees so you must take giant steps to walk through the snow. Finally you are home, and just in time! The snow is as deep as your head! Open the

door and go inside. Take off your hat, your mittens, your coat, and your boots. Now snuggle down with a blanket and take a sip of hot cocoa.
- Make little snowmen. Stack snowballs on a plastic plate. Decorate with buttons, twigs and scraps of cloth.
- White board patterned sentences:
    I wear my coat on a snowy day.
    I wear my boots on a snowy day.
    I wear my gloves on a snowy day.
    I wear my scarf on a snowy day.
    I wear my hat on a snowy day.

Songs, Rhymes, and Rhyming Stories:

Opening: Time for Storytime (p. 47)

There Was an Old Woman Who Lived in a Shoe (p. 57)
Little Jack Horner (p. 61)
Raise Them High (p. 44)
I'm a Little Teapot (p. 66)

Closing: Goodbye for Now (p. 38)

Handouts:

Recipe: Applesauce Pancakes (see Appendix)

SPLISH SPLASH SPLOSH

Introduction

Pretend it is a rainy day. First you may hear the wind begin to blow. Then you may see the clouds covering the sky. Then you feel one little raindrop splash on your face! At first the rain falls softly. Pat your lap lightly to make the sound of the rainfall. Then the rain really begins to pour! Pat your lap harder and faster to make a fierce storm! The rain slows down, and slows down, and finally stops.

Books to Share and Extended Learning Activities

Beaumont, Karen. *Move Over, Rover.* Harcourt, 2006.

Rover is bored and alone in his dog house until thunder crashes, lightning flashes, and the rain begins to pour. Soon friends begin to pour in, too.

Literacy Features: Phonological awareness, narrative skill

Extended Learning Activities:

- Phonological awareness activity: Re-read the list of commands and emphasize the alliteration and rhyme.
    Slide aside, Snake!
    Out of the way, Blue Jay!
    Squeeze in, Squirrel!
    Make room, Raccoon!
    Skit-scat, Cat!
    Move over, Rover!
- Mark a 3' × 3' area on the floor with tape. This will be Rover's doghouse. As you turn the pages a second time, choose one child to be Rover, the cat, the raccoon, etc. See how many animals you can pack into a tight space!

Puttock, Simon. *Squeaky Clean.* Little, Brown, 2002.

Mama pig gives her grubby little piglets a bath. They squeal and squirm until she adds bubbles.

Literacy Features: Narrative skill, phonological awareness

Extended Learning Activities:

- Counting rubber ducks: Bring a dishpan with water and a few rubber ducks. Count the ducks as you plop them into the tub.
- Narrative skill and oral fluency: Ask the children to talk about what makes the best bath time ever. For example, warm water, a soft towel, a favorite toy.
- Carefully pronounce the words *squeak, squeal,* and *squirm* and invite the group to repeat. Ask "Can you think of any more words that begin the same way?" (squash, squirrel, square).

Cronin, Doreen. *Click, Clack, Splish, Splash: A Counting Adventure.* Atheneum, 2006.

While Farmer Brown sleeps, some of the animals who live on the farm go on a fishing expedition.

Literacy Features: Phonological awareness, print motivation

Extended Learning Activities:

- Point to the words click and clack on the cover. Ask "Can you think of any more words that start the same way?" (clock, clean, clap).
- Give the children 10 goldfish crackers in a paper cup. Let them count the crackers as they put them back in the cup, or eat them.
- Working together game: In this story, the animals work together to take the fish from the farmer's fish tank and release them at the shore. For a follow-up activity, get the whole group to work together to place 10 objects in a basket. Start with 10 beanbags, balls, or small toys. Start passing the toys from person to person down the row until the last person puts toys into a basket. When all 10 items are in the basket everyone cheers!

Buzzeo, Toni. *Dawdle Duckling.* Dial, 2003.

Mama Duck tries to keep Dawdle Duckling together with his siblings, but he wants to dawdle and dream, preen and play, splash and spin.

Literacy Features: Vocabulary, narrative skill

Extended Learning Activities:

- To teach the meaning of the word dawdle, ask each parent and child team to walk from one end of the room to the other. Most of the teams should walk fast, but the last team should walk slowly, zigzagging and stopping to tie their shoes or point to objects in the room. Everyone should call out, "Quack! Catch up!"
- Ask the children why Mama Duck wanted all of her ducks to stay close. Was there something dangerous in the water? What was it?

Sample Storytime Plan

Theme: Splish Splash Splosh—fun with water

Presentation Dates: _____

Literacy Skill Focus: Phonological awareness

Books:

Move Over, Rover by Karen Beaumont
Click, Clack, Splish, Splash: A Counting Adventure by Doreen Cronin

Extended Learning Activities:

- Phonological awareness activity: Re-read the list of commands in *Move Over, Rover* and emphasize the alliteration and rhyme.
  Slide aside, Snake!
  Out of the way, Blue Jay!
  Squeeze in, Squirrel!

> Make room, Raccoon!
> Skit-scat, Cat!
> Move over, Rover!

- Point to the words click and clack on the cover. Ask "Can you think of any more words that start the same way?" (clock, clean, clap).
- Working together game: In this story, the animals work together to take the fish from the farmer's fish tank and release them at the shore. For a follow-up activity get the whole group to work together to place 10 objects in a basket. Start with 10 beanbags, balls or small toys. Start passing the toys from person to person down the row until the last person puts toys into a basket. When all 10 items are in the basket everyone cheers!

Songs, Rhymes, and Rhyming Stories:

Opening: Time for Storytime (p. 47)

Someday I Would (p. 45)
Two Little Black Birds (p. 62)
Five Baby Dragons (p. 70)

Closing: Goodbye for Now (p. 38)

Handouts:

Two Little Black Birds finger puppets (p. 62) or Someday I Would song sheet (p. 45)

WHAT'S FOR LUNCH?

Introduction

Let the children help you set the table. Spread a tablecloth or use two placemats. Then let them set plates, cups, napkins, and silverware. Ask them to imagine the best lunch ever. What kind of food would they have? Ask the adults in the room to tell their favorite food to eat for lunch.

Books to Share and Extended Learning Activities

Newman, Leslea. *Pigs, Pigs, Pigs.* Simon and Schuster, 2003.

The whole town prepares for their guests who are coming by bus, train, plane, and hot-air balloon. The pigs devour a huge meal and then put on a show.

Literacy Features: Vocabulary

Extended Learning Activities:

- Vocabulary and narrative skill: Talk about the kind of transportation that the pigs employed to get to the feast. Ask the children to think of some other means of travel (on horseback, riding a camel, a school bus, etc.).
- Pig Out! On the magnet or flannel board, place pictures of favorite kid foods and start a discussion about the foods they enjoy pigging out on (pizza, macaroni and cheese, tomato soup, spaghetti, etc.).

Harris, Trudy. *20 Hungry Piggies.* Millbrook, 2006.

Twenty pigs have been invited to a picnic. The wolf arrives, hoping for a pork chop meal, but when the twentieth pig rings the dinner bell, a pig stampede saves them all.

Literacy Features: Vocabulary, phonological awareness

Extended Learning Activities:

- See if the children can spot the sneaky wolf throughout the book.
- Look for the number on the pig and also hidden somewhere on the page.

Fleming, Denise. *Lunch.* Henry Holt, 1992.

It is time for lunch, and one hungry little mouse devours a feast of colorful foods, and then takes a nap until dinnertime.

Literacy Features: Vocabulary, print motivation

Extended Learning Activities:

- Encourage the children to guess what fruit or vegetable mouse will eat next; pause before turning the page.
- Make a list of the children's favorite foods and colors. Write them on the white board. If possible, use the corresponding color of marker to write them. For example, RED TOMATO, GREEN SPINACH, PURPLE PLUM.

Mazer, Norma Fox. *Has Anyone Seen My Emily Greene?* Candlewick, 2007.

It is time for lunch, and Emily's father has prepared noodles, ham, and fresh-baked bread. But he cannot find Emily Greene! He searches everywhere. Finally there is a knock at the door. Who can it be?

Literacy Features: Phonological awareness, narrative skill

Extended Learning Activities:

- On the second reading, ask the children to tell you where Emily Greene is hiding as her father looks behind the door, under the rug, etc.
- Emphasize the rhymes as you read, for example door, floor, roar.

Tekavec, Heather. *What's That Awful Smell?* Dial, 2004.

The animals in the barn are trying to find the cause of an awful smell. Could it be the piglet? Or did one of the animals hide their smelly lunch in the barn?

Literacy Features: Vocabulary, print motivation

Extended Learning Activities:

- The best sandwich; the worst sandwich: Ask the children to give you their favorite sandwich combinations. Then ask them to think of the most terrible, smelly, awful sandwich. For example: sauerkraut, onions, garlic, and salami with chocolate sauce.
- What do the animals like to eat? Ask the children to discuss what animals like to eat. For example, chickens like corn, cows like grass, dogs like bones.

Sample Storytime Plan

Theme: What's for Lunch?—imagine the best lunch ever

Presentation Dates: _____

Literacy Skill Focus: Vocabulary

Books:

> *Lunch* by Denise Fleming
> *What's That Awful Smell?* by Heather Tekavec

Extended Learning Activities:

- Vocabulary activity: Ask the group to name lunch foods, including fruits, vegetables, grains, etc.
- The best sandwich; the worst sandwich: Ask the children to give you their favorite sandwich combinations. Then ask them to think of the most terrible, smelly, awful sandwich. For example: sauerkraut, onions, garlic, and salami with chocolate sauce.
- White board activity: Make a list of the children's favorite foods and colors. Write them on the white board. If possible, use the corresponding color of marker to write them. For example, RED TOMATO, GREEN SPINACH, PURPLE PLUM.

Songs, Rhymes, and Rhyming Stories:

> *Opening:* Time for Storytime (p. 47)

> My Meals (p. 42)

Pizza Popcorn Peanuts (p. 43)
Way Up in the Apple Tree (p. 67)
Mouse Goes Out (p. 72)

Closing: Goodbye for Now (p. 38)

Handouts:

Recipe for Peachy Peanut Pita Sandwich or Bunny Rabbit Salad (see Appendix)

Recipes and Resources

EASY FAMILY RECIPES

Scented Colored Play Dough

1 cup cold water
1 tbsp. oil
1 package unsweetened flavored drink mix

1/4 cup salt
1 cup flour
5 tsp. cream of tartar

In a heavy saucepan, combine water, oil, drink mix, and salt. Heat and stir until salt is dissolved. All at once, add flour and cream of tartar. Cook over medium heat until mixture forms a ball. Remove from heat. Remove dough from saucepan and cool on a cookie sheet. Knead the dough when it is cool enough to handle. Store in plastic bag or plastic container with a tight-fitting lid.

Sparkling Snow Play Dough

2 cups water
2 cups flour
1 cup salt

4 tsp. cream of tartar
4 tsp. oil
iridescent glitter

Combine ingredients in a heavy saucepan. Cook over medium heat, stirring constantly with wooden spoon until mixture thickens and pulls away from sides of pan. Form dough into a ball and place on a cookie sheet to cool. Knead in glitter. Store in plastic bag or plastic container with a tight-fitting lid.

Bathtub Paint

6-cup muffin tin
spoon

can of shaving cream
food coloring in several colors

Squirt shaving cream into each section of muffin tin. Add a few drops of food coloring and stir with a spoon.

Bunny Rabbit Salad

4 pear halves
lettuce
4 ounces softened cream cheese
1 tbsp. milk

raisins
flaked coconut
carrot

Place pear halves cut side down on lettuce leaf. Stir milk and cream cheese together. Spread cream cheese mixture over the pears. Use raisins for eyes, thin slices of carrots for the ears and coconut for the fur.

English Muffin Pizza

2 English muffins, split in half
4 ounces pizza sauce

1 cup grated mozzarella cheese
olives, pepperoni, or Canadian bacon

Place English muffin halves on cookie sheet. Spread with pizza sauce. Top with cheese. If desired, add olives, pepperoni, or Canadian bacon. Bake at 450°F for 12 minutes or until cheese is melted.

Peachy Peanut Pita Sandwich

2 pita breads
1/4 cup crunchy peanut butter
1 fresh peach, peeled and sliced

Cut open pita bread. Warm for 15 seconds in microwave. Spread with peanut butter. Add sliced peaches.

Applesauce Pancakes

2 cups dry pancake mix
1 tsp. cinnamon
2 eggs

1 cup applesauce
1 tsp. lemon juice
1/2 cup milk

Mix all ingredients in large bowl, stirring just until moistened. Heat a griddle until drops of water bounce. Spray griddle with cooking spray. For each pancake, pour 1/4 cup pancake mix onto griddle. Bake until bubbles begin to break. Flip once. Bake one minute longer. Serve with maple syrup or apple butter.

Oatmeal Raisin Cookies

2/3 cup sugar
2/3 cup packed brown sugar
1/2 cup butter, softened
1/2 cup butter shortening
1 tsp. baking soda

1/2 tsp. baking powder
1/2 tsp. salt
2 large eggs
3 cups old-fashioned or quick-cooking
   oats

| 1 tsp. ground cinnamon | 1 cup all-purpose flour |
| 1 tsp. vanilla | 1 cup raisins |

Preheat oven to 375°F. Mix all ingredients, except oats, flour, and raisins, in a large bowl. Stir in oats, flour, and raisins. Drop dough by rounded tablespoonfuls 2 inches apart onto an ungreased cookie sheet. Bake 9 to 11 minutes or until light brown. Immediately remove from cookie sheet to a wire rack for cooling.

BILINGUAL BOOKS—PUBLISHERS, LISTS, AND RESOURCES

ALA list of bilingual books. www.ala.org/ala/alsc/alscresources/booklists/bilingualbooks .htm (accessed July 14, 2008). Published between 1995 and 1999 and currently in print.

Bilingual Books. www.bilingualbooks.com (accessed July 14, 2008). Resource for bilingual English/Spanish materials for children and adults. Includes rhymes, myths, fables, songs.

Bilingual English/Somali picture books list. www.minnesotahumanities.org/Bilingual/ somalipicturebooks.pdf (accessed August 5, 2008). Compiled by Minnesota Humanities Commission.

Culture for Kids. www.cultureforkids.com (accessed August 5, 2008). The Culture for Kids mission is to be the best global resource for teaching about languages and cultures. They review thousands of products and choose only the best quality.

Essential Espanol. www.ingrambook.com (accessed October 12, 2008). Ingram's monthly online publication, annotated in English for most titles.

Global Language. www.globallanguage.com.au/new/index2.htm (accessed August 7, 2008). Publishes bilingual books for children in 55 languages.

Vietnamese Artwork. www.vietnameseartwork.com (accessed July 15, 2008). Online book store with Vietnamese/English children's books.

Index

Page numbers followed by the letter "f" indicate figures.

About the Author

Kathryn Totten lives in Littleton, Colorado. She is the manager of Thornton Branch and Outreach Services for Rangeview Library District in Thornton, Colorado, and is a former foreign language teacher. She is a member of the ALA Subcommittee on Bookmobiles and the Association of Bookmobiles and Outreach Services. She has presented on early childhood literacy and storytimes at state and national conferences.